"Every boy grows up with questions about comic books: Who's better, Batman or Superman? Who would win in a fight, Wolverine or Magneto? Travis Smith grew up and is now asking intellectually serious questions about comic books: Who is a better representative of idealism in action--Captain America or Mister Fantastic? Who better embodies the human capacity for imagination—Green Lantern or Iron Man? Travis is a nerd's nerd and *Superhero Ethics* is fun and engaging. If you've ever cared about comic books or superheroes, you'll love it."
    —**JONATHAN V. LAST**, digital editor, the *Weekly Standard*

"Travis Smith ably demonstrates that costumed characters have a bigger purpose in our modern world than just filling movie studios' coffers. If you look closely—and Smith really has—they can teach us plenty about right and wrong in these morally murky times."
    —**REED TUCKER**, author of *Slugfest: Inside the Epic, 50-Year Battle Between Marvel and DC*

"*Superhero Ethics* cleverly casts famous superheroes against each other and compares their ethics in an enlightening and enjoyable fashion, and in doing so emphasizes the true value of superheroes in society today."
—**MARK D. WHITE**, chair of the Department of Philosophy at the College of Staten Island/CUNY and the author of *The Virtues of Captain America: Modern-Day Lessons on Character from a World War II Superhero*

"*Superhero Ethics* reminds us to look beyond the powers of superheroes to see their important role as models of personal responsibility, accountability and integrity, of being willing to wrestle with moral and ethical issues, and to work in the service of others."

—ROBIN S. ROSENBERG, clinical psychologist and author
of *Superhero Origins: What Makes Superheroes Tick
and Why We Care*

"Part *Plutarch's Lives*, part conversation with a friend from the local comic book store, *Superhero Ethics* is one of the freshest and most interesting books I have ever read on the contemporary relevance of superheroes."

—ADAM BARKMAN, professor of philosophy,
Redeemer University College

"A quirky, accessible, and thoughtful account of whom we should emulate: Spider-Man, Batman, Wolverine, Hulk, Superman, and others. A delightful read and a thought-provoking analysis"

—LEE TREPANIER, professor of political science,
Saginaw Valley State University and editor of the
Levington book series, *Politics, Literature, & Film* series

"Myths possess a moral content that helps define our values. In *Superhero Ethics*, Travis Smith examines one neglected source of modern myths—"comic-book" stories of do-gooders with great powers—and discloses their many insights about the good life and its great responsibilities."

—JOHN M. PARRISH, professor of political science,
Loyola Marymount University

"In *Superhero Ethics*, Travis Smith employs his deep learning about political philosophy to illumine the various worlds of comic-book heroes, which he shows is much richer than one might be inclined to think. He writes with passion, intelligence and wit on a subject he manifestly cherishes: a true labor of love."

—**STEVEN J. LENZNER**, Henry Salvatori Research Fellow in Political Philosophy, Claremont McKenna College

"Implicit in our childhood debates over superheroes are arguments about which kind of life is best for us as mere mortals. In this delightful work, Travis Smith puts our arguments to the test, pitting superhero against superhero in a titanic clash over the nature of the good life."

—**JOEL JOHNSON**, professor of government, Augustana University

SUPERHERO ETHICS

SUPER HERO

ETHICS

10 COMIC BOOK HEROES
10 WAYS TO SAVE THE WORLD
WHICH ONE DO WE NEED
MOST NOW?

Travis Smith

TEMPLETON PRESS

Templeton Press
300 Conshohocken State Road, Suite 500
West Conshohocken, PA 19428
www.templetonpress.org

Set in Dante MT Std by Gopa & Ted2, Inc.

Library of Congress Control Number: 2018940362
ISBN: 978-1-59947-454-0 (cloth: alk. paper)

This paper meets the requirements of ANSI / NISO Z39.48-1992
(Permanence of Paper).

A catalogue record for this book is available from the
Library of Congress.

18 19 20 21 22   10 9 8 7 6 5 4 3 2 1

Printed in the United States of America.

For Katie Ditschun

Well now I'm no hero that's understood
—BRUCE SPRINGSTEEN

And then a hero comes along
—MARIAH CAREY

Contents

Acknowledgments

WITHOUT the expert guidance of Sonny Bunch, this book would probably still be in draft form on my hard drive. Thank you, Sonny, for helping me to bring the pieces of this project together and make an integrated, coherent whole out of them, and for your good sense regarding what should and shouldn't make the final cut. Without Susan Arellano, this book would never have come to be. Thank you, Susan, for your constant encouragement and for continuing to believe in this book through sundry snags and delays. My gratitude extends to Angelina Horst, Daniel Reilly, and Trish Vergilio, the entire team at Templeton Press, and the John Templeton Foundation. Adam Bellow, William Kristol, Jonathan V. Last, and Peter Stockland all contributed to creating the opportunities that brought this book into being. Many conversations with colleagues, students, family, and friends have provided me with invaluable assistance in its preparation. I would personally like to extend my appreciation to Samuel Ajzenstat, Paul Allen, Justin Ballard, Adam Barkman, Dejai Barnes, Mike Campol, Jarrett Carty, Jason Ferrell, Jim Fitch, Matthew Flanagan, Karen P. Foster, Eli Friedland, Dónal Gill, Joel A. Johnson, Geoffrey Kellow, Steven J. Lenzner, Jacob T. Levy, Ryan McKinnell, Sibbyl Nickerson, José Daniel Parra, Anna F. Peppard, Jeremy Prince, Taylor Putnam, Lex Resnick, and Ian Smith. My wife, Kate, bless her soul, has proofread every page more than once. I am indebted to my son, Alexis, for more than a couple of arguments, and to my parents, Larry and Brenda, who stored my comic book collection in their basement for many years. The Department of Political Science at Concordia University, the College of the Humanities at Carleton University, the Canadian Political Science Association, and the Canadian Society for the Study of Comics have provided me with venues at which to give my ideas a try. To all of the artists, writers, publishers, actors, and filmmakers who have told the stories that provided the raw material for my analyses, thank you for your inspiration. Meanwhile, Alex La Prova and Rob Rossi at Major Comics on Rue Pierce in Montreal have supplied me with my weekly fix every Wednesday. I am wholly responsible for any errors of fact or judgment contained in this book. If anyone listed above should find my labor generally decried, they may be pleased to excuse themselves.

SUPERHERO ETHICS

INTRODUCTION
Challenge of the Superheroes

WHICH SUPERHERO IS BEST?

O N SCHOOLYARDS, in comic book shops, at movie theaters, and all over the Internet, people quarrel over which of our costumed crusaders is supreme. But determining which man, mutant, or alien is the most impressive of them all requires us to first define our terms. What does it even mean to be "best" in this context?

Some would pick their champion by asking who would win any given fight, one-on-one. On those terms, you could make the argument that the Silver Surfer is the greatest; after all, he wields the power cosmic. But this is a troublesome measure, given the fact that virtually any hero can triumph in any given matchup, depending on the cleverness of the writer crafting the tale. Consider the fact that Marvel and DC allowed readers to vote for the winners of the main bouts in the 1996 matchup miniseries, *DC Versus Marvel*; regardless of who the voters chose, the publishers knew they could write their way to a winner. What if someone suggested that the superhero who racks up the most sales is obviously best—the market can't be wrong, can it? But that maxim meets its match when we consider that Cable—a time-traveling mutant best known for his enormous guns and extraneous pouches—would then have to be considered one of the greatest superheroes of all time. After all, the debut issue of *X-Force*, featuring the team he led, sold roughly five million copies back in 1992, putting it near the top of all-time single-issue sales.

Many people simply prefer characters who most resemble themselves, or, rather, the person they think they wish they could be. Batman attracts many fans on account of his vaunted humanity, his relentlessness and resourcefulness, and his apparent indomitability. Trends in the culture and the counterculture also play a part in deciding favorites. Lately, some characters have gained popularity because we want to see women and people of color empowered. The perception of an overbearing political correctness, however, can trigger a backlash against those very efforts. If Miles Morales, the Ultimate Spider-Man, or Kamala Khan, the new Ms. Marvel, are to retain recognition as great new characters, the reasons for rooting them on must transcend identity politics. Wonder Woman, for instance, is wondrous for reasons that exceed her womanliness. The relative status of a character within their fictional universe is another standard by which one may be measured—the immensity of the threats they face, the degree of villainy among the foes they thwart, not to mention the admiration that their fellow heroes have for them. Consider how Superman and Captain America are held up as moral exemplars within their respective universes: They are heroes even to the other heroes, like Michael Jordan is to other basketball players. Or, one might find more inspiration in those who struggle with adversity and distress on a personal scale, like Jessica Cruz, the newest Green Lantern, or Netflix darling Jessica Jones.

Instead of arguing over which character is "best," with all the amorphousness that word entails, perhaps we can narrow our focus a bit. What if, instead, we try to decide which superhero is most praiseworthy?

LOOKING FOR SOMEONE TO LOOK UP TO

This book concentrates on familiar characters and uses them to bring into focus fundamental themes about the human condition. We will examine the ways that they embody major ethical issues, consider how well they represent our highest ideals, and ask whether they should serve as models for admiration and emulation. We will compare their merits and the qualities they represent in an endeavor to determine which one of them best serves as a model of good character in today's social and political context.

This approach means evaluating each character, the powers they possess, and the battles they wage, not literally (Does it really matter how many kilojoules Superman's heat vision expends?), but metaphorically, so that they are rendered less fantastical and more relevant to the lives of us less heroic, nonsuper beings. This means focusing more on qualities of character, on virtues and flaws, than on the intricate plots and bloated action sequences that tend to dominate on the page and on the screen—except insofar as plot and action may be revealing of character. At their worst, superhero films devolve into frenetic montages of bright lights and loud noises, featuring lots of action but little psychology. At their best, however, the remarkable attributes, incredible situations, and amazing exploits of superheroes can be read as resembling or corresponding to something in our own lives.

Some readers may complain that my attempts at identifying the essential moral qualities that constitute each character's ethical core transcend authorial intent, or even transgress against it. But works of art often exhibit different meanings and significance beyond the intention of the artist. It is also inevitable that I will have to be selective in deciding which traits to emphasize and which stories to prioritize in defining each character's distinctive qualities. These are characters about whom thousands of stories have been told by many different writers, artists, directors, and actors, across multiverses and multiple media. Their stories contain inconsistencies, even when attempts are made to respect continuity, in large part because keeping enduring characters like these fresh requires tweaking them on occasion—shifting their circumstances or altering their attributes.

I will draw upon an assortment of existing depictions in preparing my portrait of each character. Alternate representations of the same character must share some common core in order to be meaningfully identifiable as versions of that person. Even bizarro or mirror-universe inversions of characters rely on the existence of a baseline orientation on which to tilt the axis. While the interpretations I will offer of each hero may be controversial—and I trust that fans with comprehensive knowledge of these characters' histories will nitpick—we should still be able to agree that these characters possess some distinctive, fundamental qualities about which we can argue. Otherwise, we wouldn't be able to say, as fans often do when arguing with each other, that some modification to a given superhero "betrays" that character. We should know the difference between a predicament that tests or twists a superhero's character in order to see how he'll rise to a challenge or handle the aftermath in a manner consistent with his true nature (such as when Superman is possessed or mind-controlled and kills someone or when a cosmic cube turns Captain America into a fascist for a while) and times when a character betrays himself or is betrayed by those penning his adventures (say, Batman mowing crooks down via machine guns or Spider-Man making a deal with the devil). Even if you have your quibbles, I hope you'll agree that the chapters in this book accurately render each character's ethical core, the moral questions they raise, the conundrums they present, the tensions they underscore, the resolutions that they offer, and the examples they set.

MEN, NOT GODS

In order to counter the dismissal of superhero stories as mere juvenile escapism, they are sometimes treated as modern-day mythology, our version of the Greek gods doing battle on Olympus and meddling in the affairs of mortals. But overemphasizing the faux-divinity of superheroes makes them less accessible to us and less applicable to our own lives—especially in modern times, where we tend to reject divinities and demigods as role models. These characters are generally written in ways that humanize them. We are meant to find these fantastic figures relatable in some way, even if their bodies are too perfect, their costumes garish, and their adventures inherently unrealistic. When Aunt May reminds Peter Parker that "there's a hero in all of us" in *Spider-Man 2* (2004), we're supposed to feel like she's talking to each one of us sitting in the movie theater.

Superhero stories no longer need nonpowered supporting characters like Justice League mascot Snapper Carr or Green Lantern's mechanic Tom Kalmaku to play the role of the ordinary human being with whom readers could identify. Wherever that sort of character persists, such as Team Arrow's Felicity Smoak, the Hulk's sidekick Rick Jones, or S.H.I.E.L.D. Agent Phil Coulson, they tend to have extraordinary talents, too, and they are often eventually given superpowers of their own. These days, we're mainly supposed to identify directly with the superheroes themselves. Consider the way *Man of*

Steel (2013) ditched Superman's pal, Jimmy Olsen; audience members are encouraged to put themselves into the shoes of Clark Kent as he wrestles with his newly discovered identity as Kal-El.

Some readers might object that I am giving a genre that glorifies violence too much credit and that there's nothing of value to take away from stories about freaks throwing haymakers at each other. But this book is premised on the idea that it's not their super*powers* that make superheroes so super. It is their extraordinary character, their inherent qualities that make them heroic and render them worthy of praise. The powers they possess and the battles they wage can be understood symbolically, as representative of the struggles we ordinary mortals face within ourselves and out there in the world, and the means by which we strive to overcome them or cut through them. Human ethics can be related in and through superhero stories. Superheroes provide exaggerated and extraordinary representations of the qualities that human beings must cultivate in order to confront the quandaries of ordinary life. In fact, the very way that the fantastical qualities of their stories distance them from real-world struggles actually makes it easier, with a little imagination, to interpret and apply them to a range of real-world problems and experiences. Realistic accounts and concrete examples of the adversities that actual people endure often seem too particularistic, too specific to them, and therefore harder to relate to unless you share the same traits or undergo similar ordeals.

METAPHORS, NOT MESSIAHS

Emphasizing the human dimensions of the superhuman, this book asks: Which superheroes are better models for admiration and emulation by us in our circumstances today? We will find in the course of this questioning that some heroes represent qualities we should avoid cultivating in ourselves. Not every superhero is worthy of great admiration and emulation—and I'm not referring only to those who are overtly morally ambiguous, such as the Punisher or Midnighter, or those who blatantly mock the assumption that there should be anything morally salutary about superheroes, such as Deadpool or Harley Quinn.

Treating superheroes as role models is unlikely to inspire tremendously heroic efforts from ordinary human beings. That's probably for the best anyway; a night watch of would-be vigilantes bedecked in hockey pads pummeling muggers is likely to lead to more trouble than it's worth. But freedom well used ought to spark some virtue, some relative excellence of character. So if superheroes can encourage some everyday ethical behavior—inspiring responsibility and integrity, living with resolve rather than resignation—while exposing some of our worst tendencies and misguided aspirations, then it is worth thinking about them critically. The happiness of individuals and the well-being of a free society depend in part upon people behaving responsibly: Too many forces in our liberal democratic society today already inculcate irresponsibility, promote narrow self-interest and hedonistic indulgence, and foster sentimentality and wishful thinking. Our society too often sanctions timid passivity and outsized outrage—all in the name of compassion or justice. We either discourage or downplay everyday bravery, moderation, restraint, resilience, generosity, gratitude, decency, sociability, sacrifice, the exercise of good judgment, and the development of intellectual prowess—all of the efforts that generate and constitute responsibility toward oneself and one's community. Personal responsibility almost seems supererogatory nowadays. People instead clamor for "collective responsibility"—by which they too often mean "other people should do it and pay for it."

Now, a yearning for real-world superheroes, speaking literally, would concern me. We are already too eager to follow charismatic leaders who promise to save us and fix everything for us. But treating superheroes as metaphors turns them into examples of power and freedom that we can use to improve our own lives. Cultivating responsibility in others and ourselves is our duty, and this is done not only by providing living examples to emulate but also by telling stories to educate; we are more receptive to analogies than commands. This is the power of great literature, and while Stan Lee may not rest on the same plane as Cervantes or Shakespeare, these artists are pursuing similar goals. Despite perennial accusations of their basic vulgarity, the present popularity of superhero stories can be seen as heartening. Their attractiveness indicates that some appreciation remains within us for the kinds of lessons that they tend to communicate. There is something about their ethical appeal that is ineradicable despite prevailing tendencies within the broader culture to denigrate or dismiss ethical imperatives. Stories, in short, are powerful—perhaps even superpowerful.

Who Ya Got?

No list of characters in a book like this would ever satisfy every fan—and this particular fandom is notorious for virulent bickering over exceedingly trivial affairs. My principal consideration while choosing the ten champions who face off against one another here was whether I could present each of them as exemplifying some important ethical concern or perspective.

I don't include the Flash, for example, because, I confess, his ethical significance remains something of a mystery to me. (It's something to do with our mortality, our finitude, I think.) Also, for the sake of providing contrast and avoiding overlap, the contribution of each character has to be sufficiently distinctive. I do not include Captain Marvel (Carol Danvers) because I include Wolverine, with whom she shares the refusal to self-identify as a victim despite having been regularly victimized. I do not include Green Arrow because I include Batman. Because I was already considering Captain America, I didn't include Black Panther—although 2018 has deservedly raised awareness of the Wakandan king. I have avoided characters whose origin stories are dependent on another character; otherwise I would have written about Supergirl rather than Superman, as she is more interesting and more complicated, ethically speaking. I forced myself to set aside my own idiosyncratic personal favorites; otherwise I would be spotlighting Squirrel Girl and Booster Gold. Also, to make sure this book is accessible to general audiences, I felt the need to focus on characters with greater mainstream name recognition rather than obscurities beloved only by hardcore fanboys and -girls. Thus, all of the characters under consideration have appeared in feature films within the past decade. Finally, there has to be a rich-enough tradition built up around each character for me to have enough to say about them, as well as sufficient resources to draw upon in backing up my claims. The newest character among those I have included, therefore, is Wolverine, who first appeared all the way back in 1974.

The book proceeds via a series of contests: The ten heroes I have chosen are paired up against each other, judged as to which is most praiseworthy in our current moment—and then one moves on. The matchups, far from random, are based on categorical commonalities with respect to some aspect of the human condition. The book concludes with an ethical battle royal of sorts, in which the victors of the preceding chapters are thrown together and forced to make the case as to which of them you, the humble reader, should model your life after. Granted, other characters might be more praiseworthy under different circumstances and different regimes. But we are concerned with the here and now. Who can serve as an example for us all? Which character's character should we seek to cultivate in ourselves today?

Approaching superheroes in this way is intended to help us to engage in some critical self-reflection regarding present-day values and trends. Superheroes represent a challenge to our egalitarian commitments. They remind us that some people in this world are in desperate need of help, while others have the capability to provide that help. We tend to be wary of claims to excellence or nobility, but we remain dependent on and continue to esteem people who exhibit superior qualities and behave honorably. The very people who warn against elitism will express uncritical adulation for audacious leadership. Superhero stories further raise the question of whether the help that people need should come from extraordinary individuals rather than the impersonal but superpowerful state. They compel us to marvel at people who feel obliged to take risks on behalf of others. They might further lead us to wonder what makes us worthy of their sacrifices.

My analyses proceed from a consideration of what is most animal about us, ascending to a consideration of what some would call most akin to the divine. As a result, the first chapter contains a consideration of two superheroes who represent and resemble what is most beastly in us: the Hulk and Wolverine. Both struggle to contain an animalistic rage that can be extremely dangerous to those around them: one by isolating himself from humanity, the other by isolating the urges within himself.

In chapter two, Iron Man and Green Lantern go head to head. They represent willpower and imagination, aspects of the human condition that are not exactly rational in themselves, but with which our reason is always engaged, either to coach or to curb. Both Tony Stark and Hal Jordan can create almost anything they can imagine—an impressive talent to possess, but a dangerous temptation, too, especially if he who wields it believes he is uniquely outfitted for reshaping the world so as to strip it of its problems.

Third, I compare two heroes who focus on our moral and social roles as residents of cities and members of communities, where we ought to find ourselves obliged to look out for each other and contribute to the common good: Batman and Spider-Man. Should we look up to somebody who believes he can improve himself to the point of mental and physical perfection in an effort to stop all crime? Or should we admire the individual who thinks he can best aid his neighborhood in smaller, simpler ways?

My penultimate chapter considers two models of the best life for human beings according to the classical tradition—the active life and the contemplative life. Captain America personifies the coincidence of moral principle and practical wisdom in action. Mister Fantastic represents the contemplative life's pursuit of wisdom for its own sake—though, obviously, a version of that life suited for the denizen of a comic book universe, one filled with ominous threats to nullify and diabolical villains to outwit in addition to equations to solve and unknowns to survey.

The final chapter will consider two characters who embody

conceptions of the divine: Thor and Superman. Thor is a pagan deity, and a prince among gods to boot. What can this astounding being of highborn privilege from a realm steeped in old-timey traditions have to teach citizens of modern liberal democratic societies? Superman is grounded in the biblical tradition, duly accentuated by the modern belief in progress. At a time when many of us are worrying whether the arc of history is bending in the right direction, his message of hope might be just what we need.

Finally, in the conclusion, we will reassess the prevailing superheroes and ask ourselves to consider just what, exactly, we want from both our society and ourselves. Which model of living is not only desirable but also feasible? Who can help us be the best we can be?

Despite their reputation as puerile amusements, superheroes are manifestations of aristocratic ideals within a liberal democratic culture. They appeal to us without simply flattering us; they offer us critical lenses with which to assess ourselves without condemning us; they recommend to us the enlargement of our sympathies and the elevation of our principles. This book considers superheroes in light of this complex set of considerations as we look to them for standards of goodness and models of excellence relevant to our times. Perhaps the optimistic, even comical, outlook that superhero stories represent—amidst an endless series of disasters and catastrophes—can provide us with some reason for hope that we still can do a decent job of being decent people, even if good never triumphs over evil permanently.

1

The Best of the Beastly

The Hulk versus Wolverine

ARE WE NOT MEN?

LET'S COMPARE the two most popular heroes among those whose superhuman qualities may be described as bestial: the Hulk and Wolverine. These two heroes, especially beloved by adolescent readers of comics and younger viewers of cartoons, represent the need to preserve our humanity despite the animal that resides within us all—as well as the secret desire to set that beast loose on occasion. They demonstrate the need to accept personal responsibility for our behavior regardless of what has happened to us; they also serve as cautionary tales about the onslaught of technological power unleashed by modern science.

Modern moralizing often treats us like pure spirits only incidentally embodied, abstracting away concrete circumstances and real-world consequences as we aspire to some theoretical ideal. For human beings to be oriented rightly toward honor, however, there needs to be an honest appreciation of our condition as animals of a sort—and an honest examination of the ways we restrain our animalistic tendencies in order to give society a chance to flourish. Our existence is inherently precarious: We live in a dangerous world where risk-taking cannot be avoided and guts aren't optional. Modern society tries to render courage unnecessary, or even dangerous; consider the standard advice given to those waylaid by a mugger: Simply hand over your belongings. People who stand their ground and defend themselves against threats are assumed to have been itching for trouble. We tend to eye those who exemplify or admire courage with suspicion, seeing them as jerks and dolts angling for a fight, putting us all in harm's way.

As we will see, Wolverine's need to defend the innocent and act honorably in a social setting contrasts with Bruce Banner's desire to live separately from society, protecting others by isolating himself from stimuli that might engage his rage. Wolverine is a heroic character with beastly qualities, fighting in a fashion that seems barbaric. The Hulk is a beast whose heroism often comes incidentally or accidentally. Wolverine will start a brawl whereas the Hulk is just really good at stumbling into one. The Hulk is practically invulnerable, thus diminishing the possibility for heroism during his rampages; he makes few sacrifices, scarcely takes risks, and requires courage only rarely. Wolverine reminds us that heroism is bloody and heroes get bloodied.

Wolverine accepts that violence is a permanent problem and he is ready for it, even on behalf of others. Honorable persons who step up in defense of others may find some pleasure in the fighting, but they don't fight for the pleasure of it. Counterintuitively, the Hulk represents the desire to avoid fighting, the wish that heroism wasn't called for. He fights out of anger and indignation that he isn't just left alone, retaliating against those who disturb him. The same people who expect everybody else to play nice can turn nasty when their peace and quiet is disturbed.

So who is more admirable? The man who struggles to restrain his animalistic nature by fighting for the rest of us in as honorable a way as he can manage? Or the man who means to repress his savagery, hoping to avoid anything that might trigger his anger and harm those unlucky enough to be nearby?

[D]ANGER

Bruce Banner, aka the Hulk, was among the first of the great Marvel characters introduced during Stan Lee and Jack Kirby's flurry of creativity in the early 1960s. Debuting in *The Incredible Hulk* in 1962, Lee and Kirby initially envisioned the Hulk as a Jekyll/Hyde archetype adapted to the circumstances of the nuclear age: Banner gains super strength, invulnerability, and strange coloration after being belted by gamma rays during the test of an experimental superweapon. Originally, the change from Banner to Hulk occurs with nightfall; in time, anger becomes the trigger that mutates the mild-mannered scientist into a superpowerful rage monster.

The shift is an important one in the Hulk's development, one that makes him more relatable. Everybody—especially Jack McGee, the tabloid reporter hot on the monster's trail in the television adaptation of *The Incredible Hulk*—knows that anger is a major theme in Hulk stories. The title sequence for the television series, which ran from 1977 to 1982, started with a red sign flashing the word ANGER, revealed to be the greater part of DANGER upon zooming out. In the comics, the Hulk undergoes regular shifts in both hue and personality. Sometimes he is more timid and tame, and other times he is more oafish and cantankerous. Sometimes he talks like a toddler; sometimes he is shrewd; and sometimes Banner's mind asserts itself fully. He has shifted from gray to green and back so many times it's hard to keep track. But the version most familiar with TV and film audiences represents the core of the character, the default to which all other variations eventually revert.

It is that version—the invulnerable, green-skinned simpleton who is "the strongest one there is"—that will be considered throughout this chapter.

The Hulk appeals to us on a visceral level: to the part of us that wishes we could lash out and smash everything; to the part that wishes everything life throws at us would bounce off harmlessly. The Hulk usually finds himself battling other monstrous creatures: often humans who have also been altered by gamma radiation, such as the Leader or the Abomination, or else aliens and extradimensional beings. Meanwhile, his personal Captain Ahab, General "Thunderbolt" Ross, hurls military materiél at him to put an end to the threat he plainly represents. The Hulk hurls it all right back. But the Hulk doesn't want to hurt anybody. Hulk just wants to be left alone! Puny humans keep trying to hurt Hulk! HULK SMASH! Once the smashing starts, the Hulk seems to relish it—like when he whips Loki around like a cat by its tail in the first *Avengers* film (2012). Eventually the Hulk will jump miles away and find a cave to hide in, leaving a dishevelled Dr. Banner to borrow some clothes and hitch a ride to the next town while "The Lonely Man Theme" plays on in the background.

Bruce Banner and the Hulk could hardly be more different. Banner, the brains, is scrawny and timid, while the brawny Hulk is fearless and dimwitted. Brilliant people are often aloof and enjoy being sequestered to focus on what really matters: the pursuit of knowledge. But scientific genius is always at risk of not getting the respect it deserves, disdained and despised by the very people who depend on it most. The Hulk represents the brainy person's desire to make ordinary people pay for underappreciating him, in physical ways that the dullards can understand.

The very name Bruce Banner sounds like Brutes Banner,

as in one who bests and bars or banishes other beasts, or else Brutes' Banner, an incomparable exemplar among brutes, suggesting that the connection between these two personae is not entirely coincidental. We have all encountered people who seem to change in an instant at the slightest provocation. Or, if we are honest, Banner harboring the Hulk within himself reminds us that we each have nightmarish qualities that we suppress in polite company.

It is said that neither gods nor beasts have a place in ordinary society. Banner himself is rather asocial, interested more in science and technology and most comfortable when cloistered in a lab. He really only values the respect of other geniuses, like his "science bro," Tony Stark. He is not the kind of guy who likes crowds or seeks the adulation of the masses. Even his inventions under the Banner Tech banner are not products for mass consumption like the stuff that Stark's corporations manufacture, but rather specialized items for extraordinary purposes. The Hulk is a recluse by nature, preferring the vast, uninhabited expanses of New Mexico. Getting away from humanity sometimes leads the Hulk on long treks to distant worlds and alternate dimensions. He never seemed more at home than on Sakaar, the world that came to be called Planet Hulk. There he became champion of its deadly arena and overthrew its despotic government with the help of a ragtag band of fellow gladiators. Back on earth, he was a founding member of the Avengers but ditched them after their first adventure together. While he rejoins the Avengers now and then during his less irrational phases, the Hulk is a better fit for the Defenders, a "nonteam" made up of other misfits like Doctor Strange, the Sub-Mariner, and the Silver Surfer. He forms alliances with aliens and other monsters, but none of his relationships endure.

The Best There Is at What He Does

The world was introduced to Wolverine in the pages of *The Incredible Hulk*: 1974's issue number 180, to be exact. Wolverine, also known as Logan, has been depicted fairly consistently over the years across all media: He's a mutant whose body rapidly self-sutures thanks to a hyperactive healing factor, which also ages him slowly; he sports sets of claws that retract into his forearms and extend on command, making their trademark *"snikt"* sound as they emerge; and, as a result of his unwilling participation in an experiment overseen by a clandestine branch of the US military, his skeleton is coated in an unbreakable metal alloy called adamantium.

Despite its impractically bright colors, Wolverine has among the most realistic costumes in comics insofar as it, like Hulk's purple pants, is often in tatters. Wolverine was introduced as the third man in a fight between the Hulk and the cannibalistic creature called Wendigo, establishing from the get-go that however beastly Wolverine seems, it is principally beastliness itself that he contends against. Nonetheless, he is renowned for his animalistic qualities. He has keen senses suitable for hunting and tracking, deadly retractable claws, and a killer's instinct that, when provoked, will send him into a "berserker rage." Even his hair is wild: Two tufts spin up above the ears, suggesting ears pricked up at danger, while bushy sideburns creep down toward his chin, and rarely is he bereft of stubble. His hirsute nature speaks to the animal ready to burst forth at any moment. Proving that he is a man, and not just some animal—especially to himself—is his leitmotif.

Wolverine is basically the same guy whether he is in costume or in flannel and dungarees. He sports the same devil-may-care attitude whether he is going by his original legal name, James Howlett, or his assumed name, Logan. Even when he disguises himself, barely, as Patch, you have no doubt who you're dealing with, bub. Whatever his flaws—including memories that have been tampered with and a body that has rebuilt itself innumerable times, Wolverine has a kind of integrity and authenticity to him. Given that our own memories are far from perfect, and that Wolverine's body only suffers spectacularly and gruesomely what ours undergo constantly but invisibly at a cellular level, his dramatic struggles with identity are not really that foreign to us.

Wolverine's origin used to be one of the biggest secrets in comics, revealed in hazy glimpses. We assumed it wasn't pretty, but it wasn't just that we didn't know his entire history that made him so intriguing—*he* didn't know it either. However, the profit motive guaranteed that an official account would be published inevitably, and several series—all of them too intricate and convoluted to bother with here—have since been dedicated to recounting his origins. What's important is that Wolverine did not set out to gain the powers he possesses: His genetic destiny gave him his healing abilities; antagonists took advantage of that gift to graft metal to his bones; and enemies have messed with his mind so often that it's fair to ask how much of his behavior may be properly called his own.

Like the Hulk, Wolverine leaves civilization behind on a regular basis. He will disappear to the iniquitous city of Madripoor, indulge in a jungle adventure, or take a motorcycle far northward where he can shed his civilized façade and wrestle grizzly bears. Despite these excursions into solitude, however, Wolverine feels the pull of society, the need to belong.

Whereas the Hulk doesn't want to have to deal with the puny humans who won't leave him be, Wolverine prefers subpolitical and premodern communities, as when he flees to the Arctic in an early episode of *X-Men: The Animated Series* (s01e06). He is wary of strangers, gruff with those whom he does not know, and generally unsociable—but not antisocial.

We see his sociability in the fact that he joins a great number of teams over the years. He was a founding member of Alpha Flight—the Canadian superteam that is housed within the federal government—but he didn't last long there. In the X-Men, he forms real friendships and learns to trust people, such as Nightcrawler, a saintly soul trapped in a body that looks demonic—who compares and contrasts nicely to the way Wolverine plays host to both beastly qualities and a noble spirit. In X-Force, preemptive assassination became routine as part of protecting mutantdom—his tribe—against the extraordinary threats it constantly faces. As an Avenger, he's the outsider within, the guy who'll do the dirty work that the others won't. Captain America told Wolverine in an early encounter (1986's *Captain America Annual* #8) that the Avengers would never have him; in time, Iron Man persuaded Cap to extend him an offer of membership (*New Avengers* #6, June 2005), insisting he's not a murderer.

Rather, "he's a samurai warrior." It's no wonder that ninjas—the dishonorable counterpart to samurai—are among Wolverine's most common sparring partners. Japan is Logan's true home away from home. There, nostalgic fantasies of a premodern society governed by traditions of honor rather than modern morals and legislation remain vibrant. Logan can imagine that in such a place he might fit in, even if he will never be made to feel welcome there.

PREDATORS, PREY, OR BOTH?

The Hulk is not motivated to become heroic by any sense of what is moral or noble. Trouble and danger find him frequently enough and he takes care of business, but he does not go out on patrol looking for criminals to apprehend. It is true that the Hulk has a soft spot for the weak: The presence of puppies or a beautiful woman calms him. The Hulk is largely a metaphor for our dismay at our frailty. He doesn't like to see people put in jeopardy, but he is motivated more by outrage at those who would victimize others than he is genuinely solicitous for their victims. He just wants *everyone* to be left alone.

Wolverine's sense of honor is personal. He does not defer to the standards of the communities he serves; he serves them in accordance with his own code. Admittedly, this makes it hard to distinguish his code from a subjective set of personal values. You might say that he fancies himself to belong to an imaginary community of noble warriors that includes the samurai from feudal Japan. But even if one dons a *kamishimo* and brandishes a katana, it is impossible to be a samurai in modern Western society. One can be a samurai only in a society that sanctions the role that samurai play. Wolverine maintains his code of honor despite the fact that within his social context he enjoys neither legal permission nor moral approval to execute his self-imposed obligations in the frightful fashion he does. Maybe his self-conception is misguided or ridiculous, even worthy of reproach. Read generously, he reminds us that something important has been given up in order for us to realize the way of life we now enjoy.

Gallantry is part of Wolverine's unfashionable masculinity. He assumes the role of protector for various ingénues in peril, such as Kitty, Rogue, and Jubilee. He has a different relationship with Jean Gray, whom he sees as a kindred spirit, someone else holding back an unfathomably dark rage. He calls her Jeannie, a homonym for genie, as if she might possess some magical way to ease his pain. Logan exhibits genuine compassion for those who are weak or in danger, because, as hard as it is to believe, he identifies with them. This commitment is on full display in *Logan* (2017), where he devotes himself to his ailing father figure, Charles Xavier, and his unexpected sort-of daughter, Laura. Bruce Banner, by comparison, tends to keep clear of relationships in which he would be obliged to care for anyone long-term. His professional relationships are shaky, and as regards women, the introverted Bruce Banner really only has his clumsy, ill-advised, and ill-fated relationship with Betty Ross—and she is better off without him.

There is some ambiguity about the heroic status of both Hulk and Wolverine; their very appearance gives that away. The Hulk was originally gray—and he sometimes turns gray again for a while—in a world where "shades of gray" suggest moral ambiguity. Even in his more familiar green and purple, the Hulk is coded as ambiguously heroic: Traditionally, superheroes wear primary colors and villains wear secondary colors. Wolverine originally and currently wears yellow and blue, but his costume during the time his popularity skyrocketed was orange with brown. On covert missions, he wears black and gray, like Batman—although Batman adds blue and yellow for his more kid-friendly appearances. The only other major character featured in this book who wears secondary colors is Green Lantern, and we'll discuss his ambiguities in the next chapter.

Nature versus Nurture; or, How Science Deforms

Modern scientific progress and liberal political theory are premised on concerns for self-preservation. There is a preoccupation with the body as something that needs to be relieved—or better yet improved upon—at the heart of the modern project. We are so dissatisfied with the human condition that we would like to change it. And yet, such changes are often treated as monstrous in fiction. Both Wolverine and the Hulk have been transformed because of man's meddling with nature, and their reaction to this tampering can help us understand which of these characters is more admirable, ethically speaking.

The essential ethical dimension of Wolverine's story is found in his determination to take responsibility for himself, no matter his genetic fate or the abuses to which he has been subjected. This message is pithily summarized in *Logan* when he tells Laura, a girl who was genetically engineered using his DNA and trained to be a savage soldier and assassin, "Don't be what they made you." That could well be Logan's own personal motto. It's a message intended for all of us: You'll always be able to find an excuse for your transgressions and derelictions if you look hard enough; a rigorous commitment to self-control is the only responsible way to live.

In contrast, Bruce Banner becomes the Hulk as a result of his own actions: He designed the gamma bomb and exposed himself to its rays when he ran onto the test site during the countdown. Yes, Banner was trying to rescue Rick Jones, who was putzing around the blast zone, and you could say that was heroic. But it was still his own invention that put Rick in danger in the first place. You could blame the military and say that Banner was only their instrument, but even that only feeds the impulse to exculpate. Ultimately, the Hulk is the monstrous offspring of the technological mind's capacity to annihilate humankind. He was conceived, absent love, in the sterile desert, following an explosion of nuclei from a gigantic phallic apparatus that seeded the earth with invisible rays. Bruce is father to his own demon.

Banner's deformation demonstrates that we need not impute bad intentions to people in order for us to be concerned about the march of progress. Nowadays, bright young Banner types with natural aptitudes for math and science are rewarded for pursuing groundbreaking work while neglecting their education in the humanities, where better judgment and greater appreciation for moral complexity might be fostered. Bruce built the gamma bomb and then found himself aghast that it might actually kill someone—even though it is designed precisely to kill kajillions. As horrible as it can be when Wolverine kills, he does it on a human scale, for reasons such as justice and honor, or in the case of Jean Gray, mercy. Weapons of mass destruction kill impersonally and indiscriminately; they're inherently dishonorable and always involve an element of injustice.

The televised and 2008 feature film versions of the Hulk are worse with respect to the recklessness that attends the hubris of scientific genius. In those instances, Banner became the Hulk as a consequence of experimenting on himself, abandoning all standard laboratory protocol and ethical guidelines. This mad-scientist scenario suggests that we imperfect human beings, no matter how smart, can be counted on to botch any attempt at self-perfection. We will disfigure ourselves and jettison our humanity in pursuit of some posthuman dream. Wolverine's entire existence, on the other hand, is an effort to reclaim his humanity, one filled with anger at having been tinkered with sans permission, one filled with bewilderment given the extent to which his memories have been messed with. The only way for him to exercise any control over his existence is by living as decently as possible in any given moment, for a man with no past has only the present by which to judge his worth.

Wolverine's way of taking responsibility is to accept who and what he is and make the best of it, no matter what nature, misfortune, and other men have done to him. Wolverine seeks neither additional technological enhancements nor ways to remove those he has been stuck with. Consider all the ways Wolverine's mind and body have been violated: False memories have been implanted into him; liquid metal was injected into him; horrific aliens have impregnated him. He's a victim who sympathizes with other victims without identifying as a victim. Wolverine does not allow victimhood to define or defeat him, even though he won't pretend it isn't a daily struggle. Given that the human condition is such that we are all victims of circumstance and mistreatment—some of us much worse than others, to be sure—Wolverine models the understanding that personal well-being depends on taking responsibility for the kind of person we will become, even though we are not at fault for the ways others have harmed us. He also encourages us to help others learn to empower themselves. To treat others as though their experiences have deprived them of agency is not actually compassionate; it only dehumanizes them further and deepens their misery.

ROUGH MEN READY TO DO VIOLENCE

Our society strongly disapproves of violence, to the point of sometimes forgetting that hostilities cannot always be averted. Bruce Banner and Logan both have very different yet strangely similar experiences with violence: They routinely flee society to avoid being mired in it, yet they both find themselves regularly caught up in it.

The Hulk speaks to our desire to be spared from maturing into civilized adulthood. He is exempt from, and takes exception to, all the niceties and compromises that polite behavior requires. Wolverine represents a pubescent fantasy of manhood that is decidedly ungentlemanly. Spirited young people stifled by a society that does not offer many opportunities for risk-taking on behalf of noble purposes are excited by him.

Wolverine allows us to live vicariously through him and sublimate our less commendable impulses. As cathartic as Wolverine's violence can be, it turns most unnerving when he loses control, especially when nefarious sorts—such as the Weapon X program, the immortal mutant Apocalypse, the terrorist group HYDRA, or ninja clan the Hand—seize control of him and turn him into a murder machine. Both Hulk and Wolverine are very violent and often mindlessly so, another reason their status as heroes is sometimes called into question.

Yet heroes they are—and conspicuous ones, at that. Both Hulk and Wolverine are exceedingly physical, fighting their foes hand-to-hand in close quarters. The Hulk's combat style has nothing graceful about it. He has never been trained in the pugilist's art. He has no need for craft when pummeling his adversaries. He is as likely to jump through a helicopter as he is to toss a tank into it from a distance. Wolverine's offense is similarly intimate and messy. The invincibility of his razor-sharp claws and his regenerative powers absolve him of the need for finesse in any scrap. Given his years of experience and training, however, Wolverine is a master of many weapons and a skilled tactician who knows how to sneak around. Still, he prefers a straight fight. Whether with his claws or samurai swords, Wolverine's weapons of choice are blades. This means that he is often drenched in blood—his opponents' and his own. Bladed weapons come to us from an earlier age: They are more honorable than handguns, more aristocratic than fisticuffs, and more elegant than both.

Wolverine's concern for honor also challenges the hedonistic side of modern society, the flipside of our idealism that suggests that what is good is simply what is pleasurable. Hedonism is an incomplete explanation for human motivation and well-being, one that cannot account for integrity, duty, or sacrifice without reducing them to some vulgar calculus. Wolverine is not cowed by pain. Indeed, he shows us the need to reject a life enslaved to the fear of pain. He accumulates no property, seeks no power, and simply enjoys what pleasures come during his downtime. The trick is to live reconciled to our animal nature without reducing ourselves to the status of mere brutes. Contrast Wolverine with his archenemy, Sabretooth—a mercenary, murderer, and worse—with comparable beastly powers and appearance but no regard for honor.

There is in Wolverine a certain scorn for modern civilization and its disregard for old-fashioned standards of honor. Given that societies governed by strict considerations of honor tend to be brutish and violent, the modern campaign against honor is not entirely unreasonable. From today's point of view, the wimpy Banner, untainted by toxic masculinity, is a good role model. Wolverine is utterly uncivilized, what with all the stabbing and slashing. But from the perspective of one primarily concerned with honor, what passes for civilization in modern times is shameless, base, paltry, cowardly, phony, and fickle. It is not something that would impress a manly man.

And if Wolverine is anything, it's manly. Cartoonishly so. The super alloy adhering to his skeleton renders his frame unyielding, just like his spirit. Wolverine's entire being is infused with the mettle of a man's man—rigid, obstinate, and indomitable. Small wonder he feels impelled to leave modernity behind now and then to wander the wilderness. Inside civilization, his etiquette is far from refined. He smokes cigars and picks fights in dive bars. His speech tends toward the surly and laconic, peppered with grunts and slang. He is, as he boasts, the best there is at what he does and what he does isn't very nice. How un-Canadian! Except he's old enough to come from a bygone Canada—a nation of beer drinkers, body checkers, and fur trappers, rugged men who entered both world wars well before the United States. Wolverine fought in those wars too. "My whole damn life is war," he says in *First X-Men* #2 (November 2012).

A more balanced perspective recognizes that modern society still depends on people having some respect for considerations of the honorable and the noble. Otherwise, liberal democracy tends to deteriorate into licentiousness or despotism, or both. Wolverine's concern for honor makes him a defender of civilization, not a deviation from it. Even though he represents an excess, if our admiration for him nudges us to have a little more respect for ourselves and for those who aspire to live honorably, that works to everyone's advantage. We just have to refrain from embracing the excesses he represents.

The Hulk represents less a criticism of modern society's excesses than a demonstration of them. He illustrates the downsides of modern individualism particularly well. Codes of honor depend on being upheld by communities that share some conception of what is noble; they are not about what is pleasing, and they are emphatically not about living free from pain and confrontation. Modern society tends instead to emphasize individuality, celebrating people who live as they please. We prefer rights to duties, bargains to sacrifices, and immediate gratification to delayed. Instead of commanding people to love one another, we say it's good enough not to harm anyone. Even when we do criticize people, it is often to stop them from criticizing other people. We would rather not bother taking an active role in bettering our neighbors' lives or serving the common good, and we would rather they let us be too.

Preferring justice to generosity or gratitude, we like entitlements from neutral, impersonal, technocratic processes, not favors from patrons. Unlike gods, human beings are not self-sufficient, but we wish we were, as evidenced by our clamor for autonomous agency, our claims to uniqueness, and our admiration for authenticity. The Hulk represents an extreme take on the idea that it would be best if we could be an island: radically independent, disentangled from relationships of obligation, and devoid of interpersonal responsibility.

SOLITUDE VERSUS SOLICITUDE

The Hulk's outlook is familiar to us from modern liberalism, with its tendency toward excessive individualism. Modern people learned to lay off and tolerate difference so that claims to love and protect each other would no longer serve as pretexts for inquisitions, persecutions, and holy wars, but the resultant individualism makes us prone to irascibility, ingratitude, intemperance, impatience, and unfriendliness. As he says in *Incredible Hulk: The End* #1 (August 2002), "Hulk doesn't want friends, because friends will hurt him. Everyone hurts him." The Hulk so wants to be alone that he dissociates from himself, speaking in the third person and reminding us regularly of how much he hates Banner.

His strength is a metaphor for how powerful we think we would be if only we were left alone. We could do whatever we want and it wouldn't harm anybody. But the view that unrestricted freedom is all that matters harbors tyrannical tendencies within it. Getting to do what one wants always involves getting others to agree, play along, and help out. That can become coercive quickly. Hence the Hulk's propensity to become a tyrant in alternate future plotlines, even though his starting point is antisocial. After all, nobody is lonelier than a tyrant.

Wolverine's motivations are nobler, but taken to an excess, they, too, can turn ugly. It's not just getting hurt that concerns Wolverine, it's being disrespected. The Hulk only understands a challenge to his physical superiority as disrespectful. Wolverine is concerned with intangibles. He wants respect and not merely to be seen as a brute. If we translate the Hulk and Wolverine onto a forum with which we are all familiar today—the Internet, where our most animalistic urges are encouraged and fulfilled—we can find analogies for the differing sorts of rage that they represent. The Hulk is like the person in a flame war who is only out to prove himself to be the smartest one there is, or superlative in some other fashion. Unwilling to budge in any argument, his only goal is to crush everybody else and stand triumphant. How dare you disagree? He will unspool furious tirades in an unremitting assault until he is satisfied that his opponents are destroyed and humiliated.

Wolverine, however, is out to protect his tribe. He takes umbrage at seeing the people with whom he identifies, or some other group in need of special protection, slighted. In a spirit of outrage, he cuts the offenders down to size for posing an existential threat. How dare you disrespect me or the tribe under my protection? Wolverine rarely flashes a smile during a fracas, but you can tell he really gets into it. Likewise, the perpetually outraged find delight in discovering the next cause to champion and another miscreant to dismantle, even if they must maintain a humorless countenance while on the attack. This impulse has its origin in presumptive righteousness, and it doesn't take long for invective to escalate into (or descend to) the online equivalent of berserker rage. One so engaged is unsatisfied until there is blood in the virtual waters and the villains are vanquished—all the while expecting, like Wolverine, to be immune from real harm. Wolverine has a nemesis in Lady Deathstrike who has powers similar to his own, but heeds a perverse code of honor gone mad. She embodies what it looks like when outrage becomes outrageous. All told, the Internet is full of the equivalent of the Hulk's roars and Wolverine's guttural growls, as we hide behind handles like masks, fancying ourselves heroes, righting wrongs worldwide, giving no quarter to the bullies and blockheads who deserve to be ripped to shreds. Civilized discourse be damned.

Now, Wolverine, like Hulk, has indeed been a victim his whole life—of nature, of circumstances, and of other people's manipulations and exploitations. Being victimized is, however, part of the universal human condition, and we must take responsibility for ourselves despite this unhappy fact. Wolverine furthermore sympathizes with others who have been badly victimized and looks out for them, potentially serving as an inspiration. I would reiterate that I am not saying victims are to blame for the harms perpetrated against them. I would add that taking responsibility for oneself does not mean assuming total control over one's life. To suppose it is possible to acquire total control is itself irresponsible, and the suggestion that a moral society involves everybody designing and executing their own Oprahesque "life-plans" is terrifying. Living with dignity involves striving for moral agency and accountability even in nonideal circumstances where total control is impossible. Because, in life, circumstances are never ideal and total control is never possible.

Wolverine's preference for premodern living fits with his awareness that his life is not something he can control. He is still determined to own it, though. Wolverine is out of place in modern society in part because modernity likes to excuse us and find others to blame for our failings. It is true that some people's circumstances are markedly worse than others'—but the only remedy for having been debased is to reassert one's dignity, despite chronic unfairness and compromised circumstances. Wolverine comes to the aid of those who have a harder time coping than he does, even though his own hardships, embodied by the alloy embedded inside him, are massive. In our world today, somebody so abused would be totally excused.

Whereas the Hulk prefers solitude, where he could theoretically enjoy his existence unmolested, Wolverine is most comfortable in a community on a smaller scale with a shared sense of goods that are worth defending. He does not have delusions of self-sufficiency; he just likes to go on the occasional vacation to get away from the vast, impersonal societies we are stuck with in modern times. Our societies boast so much power and yet devote insufficient attention to the qualities that distinguish us from mere animals that seek either simple contentment or total dominion.

Neither Banner nor Logan is overtly political. Scientific geniuses like Banner are often uninterested in politics. But in some alternate futures, the Hulk has turned into a tyrant, such as when he becomes the Maestro in 1992's *Future Imperfect*.

There he shows what happens when somebody's beastly side not only rules over themselves, but others too. Another alternate future where the Hulk becomes tyrant is shown in 2008's "Old Man Logan" storyline, where Wolverine has become utterly dispirited on account of no longer having a tribe to protect. He was in this alternate future tricked into killing the other X-Men and it has left him mostly broken. He regains his fighting spirit only after the Hulk's offspring slaughter his own small family.

Wolverine really cannot be himself unless he has a community to protect. He prefers smaller societies, which have greater potential for politics than today's immense nation-states that tend to exhibit only power plays. He is more of an auxiliary than a leader, but he is no blind follower. Whenever Logan gets put into a position of authority, like that of professor at the Xavier Institute, it is played for comic effect. But he does not hesitate to argue with those who give the orders—just ask Cyclops, longstanding leader of the X-Men.

FIGHTING IT OUT

To summarize, neither character risks much, given how hard it is to hurt the one (not counting the Hulk's feelings, which are surprisingly sensitive) and how easily the other heals (though Wolverine still endures plenty of pain; he cannot even pop his own claws without gashing his hands). One might allege that Wolverine's heroism is compromised by his healing factor insomuch as it mitigates the risks he takes—although, to be fair, all superheroes eventually bounce back from grievous injuries, if not quite as quickly as he does. Given the amount of danger and damage the Hulk causes, whatever good he and

Banner do, it is, in the end, probably a wash. Wolverine only ever intends to be the good guy but given how often he is brainwashed, he has been unwittingly made an instrument of much evil.

The Hulk represents the urge to retreat from human society in rebellion against the human condition. Wolverine represents the assertion of our distinctively human qualities in our struggle to transcend our inner animal. Bruce Banner is motivated by shame and guilt on account of suffering that he has brought upon himself and others. Logan is motivated by honor, loyalty, and a strong sense of responsibility. The Hulk throws tantrums when provoked to anger. Wolverine's motivations are less childlike and more masculine, although they are susceptible to manipulation and excess. Wolverine acts out of duty. The Hulk reacts: to pain and anger, to annoyance and abuse. The Hulk becomes more effective the angrier he gets. Wolverine's anger risks undercutting his humanity.

Bruce Banner is more heroic than the Hulk. At least he takes responsibility for his character flaws and bad judgment by working to reverse the effects of his scientific miscarriages. But Banner's efforts are primarily directed at reining in the part of himself that seeks to avoid taking responsibility. It's about reducing irresponsibility and minimizing the harm the Hulk causes. Banner is only secondarily interested in trying to make amends. If it weren't for the Hulk's mayhem, Banner wouldn't feel obliged to do much good: He would have remained the sort of technophile who takes for granted the inherent goodness of scientific discovery and technological advancement, even when it's used to do things like build bigger bombs. The cultivation of good character is often of little-to-no importance for those captivated by the siren's song of science, as we will see when we encounter Tony Stark in the next chapter.

I hesitate to declare Wolverine more praiseworthy than the Hulk if only because acknowledging Wolverine's praiseworthiness runs the risk of sounding like an apology for his lethal violence. In saying that Wolverine is more praiseworthy, I am not saying hooray for people who solve their problems with scimitars.

Wolverine finds meaning in fighting on behalf of those who require assistance. His noble aspirations prove to him—and to us—that he is a man, not an animal. Banner is about mitigating a descent into animality; Wolverine is about making an ascent from animality. Wolverine affirms the distinctively human capacity for assuming responsibility for one's own character. He reminds us that safety, comfort, and pleasure alone do not satisfy: Risk-taking, sacrifice, integrity, and aspiration—the pursuit of intangible goods like honor and virtue—are indispensable for human well-being. Neither herd animals nor predators know anything of nobility, no matter what people say about lions, elephants, eagles, and horses. Banner and the Hulk have tried to deal with the human condition by running away from it. Banner deserves credit for trying to keep his beastly side at bay, though his efforts are abortive. Other human beings, indeed all living things, remain for him a constant source of aggravation and he cannot be trusted to coexist with anyone for long. While Wolverine's animadversions against civilization are understandable, animality is his real adversary. Humanity remains his goal, and, for the sake of this argument, nothing is more praiseworthy than pushing for a higher state of being—a more noble purpose—against the temptation to fall prey to circumstances.

In short: Wolvie wins.

2

Beacons of Imagination

Green Lantern versus Iron Man

I T MAY seem odd that Marvel and DC launched their respective cinematic universes with second-tier superheroes who had no track record of success beyond their native medium, comic books, and only minor mainstream exposure in cartoons. The Marvel Cinematic Universe's *Iron Man* (2008) was massively successful, earning $585 million worldwide and kicking off a series of interconnected films grossing in the vicinity of $14 billion by the release of the third *Avengers* movie ten years later. DC's *Green Lantern* (2011) was a flop by comparison, grossing just $219 million on a $200 million budget.

The starkness of this contrast shows just how big a gamble both houses took. These were chancy beginnings to ambitious enterprises, acts of pure corporate willpower undertaken at enormous cost with gigantic fiscal implications for both parent companies. That mixture of risk-taking, resolve, and imagination is reflected in both Iron Man and Green Lantern, two characters who share a fly-by-the-seat-of-their-pants derring-do. Both are capable of crafting on-the-spot solutions to any problem, sporting a never-say-die attitude that suggests where there's a will there's always a way.

The idea that anything is possible given sufficient willpower, imagination, and means is at the core of Green Lantern and

Iron Man. It's the premise of the modern scientific and technological project too. Nothing is more emblematic of modernity than mustering imagination and questing for knowledge for the sake of acquiring useful powers, without moderating our aspirations on the basis of supposed external, objective standards regarding what is possible, permissible, and praiseworthy.

GREEN LANTERN:
WHAT WILL HE THINK OF NEXT?

There are many Green Lanterns—up to 7,200 at a time—but for this chapter I will focus on Hal Jordan, around whom the Silver Age revival of the concept was built. Created by John Broome and Gil Kane, Hal first appeared in *Showcase* #22 (September–October 1959). Green Lanterns originally gained their signature weapons—power rings devised by the Guardians of the Universe, a band of blue-skinned immortal wise men—by dint of their extreme fearlessness. Nowadays, the ability to *overcome* great fear is what is required, a description that better communicates the essence of courage.

Among its many powers, a Green Lantern ring generates protective force fields and life support, enables flight, translates alien languages, serves as a reference library, and shoots beams of energy. Fueled by willpower, it gives temporary substance to the objects of its wearer's imagination. These solid light energy constructs are used as instruments, weapons, or otherwise as needed. The shapes they take generally reflect the personality of each ring wielder: Hal traditionally made recourse to whimsical objects like giant baseball bats and fly swatters. So that they wouldn't be invincible, a Green Lantern's ring used to be vulnerable to anything colored yellow, the color of fear—an odd rule that no longer applies. Lanterns used to be incapable of employing lethal force too, but that limitation has also been lifted. Their rings now seem subject only to undefined limitations that prevent them from imparting omnipotence.

If Hal Jordan wasn't a superhero with a magic ring, he'd be bouncing from dead-end job to dead-end job—provided he hadn't gotten himself killed working as a test pilot first. He can't take care of himself, has trouble maintaining friends outside of work, and is a highly unreliable boyfriend. Being Green Lantern is the only thing Hal has ever been good at— and even then, he has lost his status as Green Lantern a few times. Hal works as a test pilot even though that's the job that killed his father; his call sign is "Highball" despite the fact that he has a DUI on his record: It is enough to make you think that his courage verges on carelessness to the point of becoming a death wish.

Why, then, did the Guardians consider him for the job? Hal's not a by-the-book space cop. He is renowned for his rebellious streak as well as for his resourcefulness—qualities the Guardians lack but require the use of. Hal's most American trait is the supposition that bravery goes together with questioning authority rather than heeding it. You get the sense that the authority of the Guardians was rarely questioned until Hal came along, save by traitors like his archnemesis, Sinestro. He questions his superiors even though he's a lowly primate from Coast City, whereas those giving the orders are cosmic beings concerned only with truth and justice, immortals with literally eons of experience backing up their judgment. The principles of freedom and equality that undergird American political life do not form the basis of the relationship between the wise Guardians and their brave auxiliaries. Hal's butting heads with the Guardians illustrates the tension between justice understood as something that protects and promotes liberty and justice understood as rational order. Freedom, in this context, is a major cause of disorder.

BILLIONAIRE PLAYBOY PHILANTHROPIST IN A CAN

Tony Stark, on the other hand, believes that his own freedom—from the limitations of the human body; from accepted ethical constraints; from laws that would prohibit private individuals from embarking upon unsanctioned international peacekeeping missions—is the best way to achieve order in a world spinning out of control.

Just as there are multiple Green Lanterns, many characters have worn Iron Man suits. For this chapter, however, I will focus on Tony Stark, who first appeared in *Tales of Suspense* #39 (March 1963). One way that Tony outshines Hal Jordan is that he manufactures his own weaponry. Constructed in a prison camp so he would survive a grievous wound and escape from foreign terrorists who demanded that he build weapons for them, his original suit was the product of ingenuity, craftsmanship, and desperate necessity. Stark's armor has served both life-saving and life-ending purposes since its inception.

Iron Man's armor has evolved as our own technology has advanced: It provides bodily protection, powers of flight, is operated by artificial intelligence, and is armed with assorted weapons and instruments, from roller skates and flashlights to sensors and repulsors. Tony builds different armors for different environments, tasks, and adversaries. He possesses the know-how and wherewithal to invent anything that might prove needful someday. Confronted by unanticipated challenges, Tony is always quick to develop a response. Even if he weren't a superhero, Tony would still be a brilliant inventor, notorious playboy, and wealthy industrialist. He suffers devastating setbacks regularly, both as a superhero and as a businessman, sometimes due to self-sabotage. Still, he always rebounds, reinvests in himself, and rebuilds his success and reputation.

There were signs of ethical ambiguity in Iron Man's character from the get-go. Before becoming Iron Man, Tony Stark made a morally dubious livelihood as an arms dealer. He is vain and ostentatious, arrogant and cocky, and unapologetically debauched. He puts his family name on all his corporate brands, inviting himself into the home of virtually everyone in the industrialized world. The Stark Expo is more lavish than the World's Fair. He forgoes his secret identity because he wants the world to know that he, Tony Stark, is Iron Man. He wants full recognition for his valiant deeds as well as for his business acumen and space-age wizardry. In *Iron Man 3* (2013), Tony attends a party wearing a name tag that reads, "You know who I am"—a gag that is not only egotistical but evocative, with both divine and diabolical connotations.

Tony trusts that he can overcome any obstacle, avert any catastrophe, and fix any problem he faces—including those he inadvertently causes. So he tends to be not all that careful. His nickname is Shellhead, suggesting a mind full of destructive force, ready to burst. Tony's faith in technology is coextensive with his faith in himself. He personifies the way the modern technological project is prepared to take great risks in pursuit of the elimination of risk. Those surrounding him react with something like bemused awe at his talents: Bruce Banner accuses Tony of heeding as a personal motto, "Let's just try things because we can" (*Avengers* #17, October 2013); in his first film, his former business partner, Obadiah Stane, describes his approach to life as "ready; aim; fire." Stark even briefly led a team in the 1990s called Force Works—a succinct way to express his creed.

With his half-Italian- and half-German-sounding name, Tony Stark sounds like the love child of an Axis Powers romance. His name roughly but fittingly translates as "powerful pre-venter," or "keen anticipator," or maybe "potent precedent." Other connotations of potency come to mind too. Sexual con-quests for a man like him are easy come, easy go, although he might consider settling down with someone he considers his equal in the boardroom and the bedroom. In Pepper Potts, he has a devoted business partner, confidante, and occasional love interest. For her own sake, however, she is best off maintaining some emotional distance from him.

PLAYING WELL WITH OTHERS

Given their status as willful outsiders, it is surprising that both Hal and Tony often find themselves having to assume leader-ship roles. Within the Justice League of America, the Green Lantern's role is on par with the Flash's: more bishop than royal. Across the universe, however, Hal Jordan is a leader within the Green Lantern Corps. He traditionally operates under the auspices of the Guardians of the Universe, although he sometimes leads in their absence, and sometimes in defi-ance of them.

Human beings used to be barred from joining the ranks of the Corps on account of being too primitive—a prejudice Jor-dan helped smash. When the ring's previous owner, Abin Sur, crash-landed on earth, his ring selected Hal to be his successor. Given how many times Hal has saved the universe, we must acknowledge that the ring made the right call. Hal has proven that he has the grit, guts, and smarts to merit membership in the Green Lantern Corps, and his proficiency on the battlefield has shown he deserves to lead it.

Tony Stark, meanwhile, is financier and often leader or cocaptain of the Avengers. He was there in 1963 when Loki's trademark mischief prompted Iron Man, Thor, Ant-Man, and Wasp to assemble to rescue the Hulk from the Trickster God's machinations. Stark was there again in 2002 at the founding of the Ultimates, a reimagined Avengers for a post–9/11 world. And, of course, the "big man in a suit of armor," as Captain American derisively describes him in the first *Avengers* film, is the center of the team in the Marvel Cinematic Universe. That said, sometimes he leaves to form splinter groups. He has frequent fallings-out with his teammates and what few friends he has and eventually has to earn back their trust over and over. Even the robots in his lab and the Artificial Intelligence in his armor—all sprung from inside Tony's head—seem to resent his existence.

Stark is perhaps an uncomfortable fit for leader of a team—he doesn't "play well with others," he admits—but that's rarely stopped him from signing on when called upon. Indeed, Stark's need to be in control, to get ahead of crises, seems ingrained in his character. He backed the government's Superhuman Registration Act in 2006's "Civil War" storyline because he thought it was better for him to be in charge than some bureaucrat; he backed the Sokovia Accords in the cinematic version of the same dispute for similar reasons.

Just *why* he needs to be in charge is another question. It is not obvious where his sense of responsibility to others comes from, what motivates him to behave heroically. Like his armor, his ethics are versatile. He doesn't espouse any pithy maxims. He doesn't swear any oaths. It is understandable that he didn't like it when bad guys tried to blow him up using weapons that his own company designed, but that doesn't explain why he goes beyond avenging himself against those who held him hostage, or those who commit industrial espionage or subterfuge against him, or those who sully his name brand by utilizing his designs for unsavory purposes. It is not clear why he fights to save the world, except insofar as that's where he keeps his high-rise, mansion, labs, and warehouses. Maybe it's just because the planet is full of people who go wild over his celebrity appearances and buy his products.

Stark seems more motivated by pleasure than honor. His tastes tend toward the more refined, but he can still be vulgar. "You can count on me to pleasure myself," he says in *Iron Man 2* (2010). He cares about fame rather than glory, yet he excels at tarnishing his own reputation. In the first *Avengers* movie, Captain America accusingly says to him, "The only thing you fight for is yourself." Even at the end of his first movie, he confesses, "I'm just not the hero type." He merely acts like one. Still, superheroism is too dangerous a hobby to take up just for the exhilaration of it. Apart from the old proverb about wanting something done right, it's not plain why Tony doesn't content himself with making a mint by manufacturing consumer goods for mass consumption and selling bespoke suits of armor to one-percenters, leaving the perilous encounters and death-defying feats to other, more heroically inclined individuals.

His mind is preoccupied with material concerns—mainly protecting his body and his property, proceeding next to protecting the lives and estates of others. In Platonic psychology, you would say that Tony has an iron soul, which makes his nom de guerre all the more appropriate. Becoming heroic is something he had to decide to do against his natural temperament and inclinations. It's something he has to work at.

Green Lantern, meanwhile, seems like the Platonic ideal of the superhero. There's a circular logic to him: If you want to know why Hal Jordan makes an excellent superhero, it is because he is exactly the kind of person who is suited to becoming a superhero. Green Lantern power rings are programmed by the Guardians to seek the best candidates to wield them. In the terms of Platonic psychology, they are looking for someone with a silver soul: someone brave who prefers the company of other brave persons, for whom membership in the Corps would be its own reward; someone with a passion for justice and an inclination to protect; someone who does not value material wealth and won't prey on others for selfish gain; someone dauntless and honest. Indeed, in Green Lantern's origin story, honesty accompanies fearlessness as a principal criterion in the selection of a recruit.

WHAT GIVES YOU THE RIGHT?

Hal's authority comes from within—he is, as we have said, chosen for his innate qualities. But he's also the wing of a paramilitary force, like the Knights Templar, in the service of cosmic truth-seekers, striving to maintain a just order within the whole of creation. Perhaps we should step back to consider Plato some more.

That Green Lantern lore borrows from Plato is suggested by the very fact that they're called the *Guardians* of the Universe. Like the philosopher-kings of Plato's *Republic*, these guardians are wise, ancient, and unchanging, busying themselves with maintaining harmonious order. They are unemotional, asexual, and without appetites. Their craniums are outsized but their bodies have largely shriveled away; all they want is to occupy themselves with contemplation, meditating together in seclusion. They react with wonder and wariness at anything new since they believe they already know nearly everything that is worth knowing. Their station is self-appointed, but they do not use it to dominate or exploit anyone. They desire neither riches nor glory and exact neither taxes nor tribute. They are not susceptible to corruption since they would not value any bribe or favor. They pursue no ideological agenda and their only partisanship is to themselves, doing what's necessary to make their lives self-sufficient.

The wisdom of the Guardians comes with incalculable power, making them seem godlike. They harnessed the essence of willpower within their Central Power Battery, from which it gets transmitted to the Green Lanterns' rings, enabling them to give form to their thoughts. Individual Lanterns are tasked with patrolling their sectors and entrusted with righting wrongs on a discretionary basis. If the threat of significant disharmony erupts somewhere, then the Guardians will send in the Corps en masse. They rarely engage personally, however, unless they are personally endangered, and then only as a last resort. They would rather not have to act at all.

The Guardians incarcerate the universe's worst offenders of justice, but they do not impose detailed legislation directly on inhabited planets. They have better things to do with their time—even though their supply of time is practically endless. Minding their own business, the Guardians mostly leave everyone free to conduct their own business. Their distant and relatively gentle touch does in fact preserve a fair degree of order across the cosmos and has done so for a long time. They do not have ulterior motives; they are genuinely concerned with truth-seeking for its own sake. As much as their presumptive superiority offends our democratic sensibilities, it really is good that they keep the Green Lanterns on a leash, and that the individuals recruited to the Corps aren't free to use their tremendous powers uninhibited, even in the name of justice.

Unlike Hal Jordan, Tony Stark derives his power entirely from his own abilities. His greatest weapon isn't his armor; it's his brain. But he is all left-brained. To him, all science is applied science, all knowledge is power. The only truths Stark cares about are useful ones. His appetite for craft knowledge is insatiable and he knows how to turn the objects of his imagination into objects that really work. He is furthermore a savvy businessman, earning billions. His genius extends beyond the boardroom too: Paired with Captain America's tactical brilliance, Iron Man is a fine battlefield strategist.

Given that there is nothing Tony Stark respects more than intellect—especially his own intellect—it is a fair question why he cares so much about ordinary people; they are, by comparison, hardly worthy of his attention. Why should he be so solicitous of the adulation of others, their being so much his inferiors?

Whatever the reason, Stark's commitment to their defense is virtually limitless. The dangers we face are legion, and so our defenses must be plentiful. Tony Stark will move from one tech to the next as weaknesses in each are exposed and superior replacements are designed. He only approximates moderation thanks to trial and error slowing him down, but in time, he will push ahead in some novel direction, implementing an entirely new platform. The technological worldview he embraces refuses to declare anything impossible, and it's never satisfied that enough has been done. It is ready to explore every avenue, deeming no experiment or operation objectionable or impermissible.

SLIPPING THE SURLY BONDS OF HUMANITY

As Jordan's ring gives him the power to transcend normal human limitations, so too does Tony's brain give him the power to transcend his very humanity. Stark is a predecessor of the modern Silicon Valley tech-head, somebody committed to transhumanism and yearning for the singularity. It's a prospect that can be traced to the philosophy of Francis Bacon, but it has only become regarded as plausible much more recently. Not that long ago, audiences understood that becoming more machine than man is twisted and evil; nowadays we covet Iron Man's means of escaping our biological limitations.

Tony went full posthuman when he invented the Extremis virus that merged his anatomy and his armor, marking the point when he unambiguously crossed the blurry line between relieving the human condition and changing human nature. Residing inside his body, his armor would emerge by mental command. You could say that instead of wearing the armor, the armor wore him. Naturally, this technology proved susceptible to being hacked or shut down by advanced artificial or alien intelligences.

Like every technological genie, the Extremis tech remains available for reuse by Tony, whether on himself or others. Meanwhile, he pursues new directions in posthuman modification. He has no concern for integrity of body or soul, only for what works. He treats his very being like his armor—as an assemblage of modular parts that can be swapped in and out, upgraded or deleted. It used to be understood that the organic was higher up the chain of being than the inorganic. Iron Man becomes more than human by melding with the less than human, demolishing any rank order of being.

Tony Stark's war against the frailty of the human body

knows no limits because it is grounded in his pride in his extraordinary intelligence and his distress at the finality of death. It is just plain stupid that a piece of shrapnel might damage his heart and cause the demise of so distinguished a mind. Seen as little more than an object with weaknesses and inefficiencies—a piece of obsolete hardware, in techie terms—the human body is impossible to understand as something that possesses inherent dignity. Iron Man represents technology's testament to our dissatisfaction with our bodies—and our excitement at the prospect of transforming them under the guise of protecting and preserving them.

Modern technology arises from within a conception of the universe that says it is made of matter in motion that obeys fixed rules. It is not chaotic, but it is without meaning or purpose. Human beings must use their imagination and willpower to impose meaning and purpose on their lives. Embracing a technological orientation to life leads us to pursue our own salvation in this world. Making ourselves ever more durable becomes our *telos* in a nonteleological universe. This is the universe as Tony Stark understands it, our place in it, and the job that needs doing.

A Guide to the Guardians

The Guardians of the Universe are aware of Tony's view of things, but they do not ultimately affirm it. For starters, their claim that Oa, the planet that serves as their base of operations, is located at the center of the universe makes no sense if the universe is expanding indefinitely and amorphously. And if we examine the Green Lantern logo, we will find that it provides a clue to understanding the Guardians' view of the cosmos.

It is a circle, bounded by parallel lines on top and bottom, circumscribed by another circle. The inner circle represents the classical philosophical view of the cosmos as an ordered whole. The universe would have to be an ordered whole for goodness and justice to have objective meaning and for nature to have inherent purposes that are discoverable. Only then may we take guidance from nature and strive to live in accordance with it. According to such a view, reality exists independently of our will and imagination, limiting how power can and should be used. This conception of reality offends our present-day sensibilities, which assert that reality is merely a social construct—a perspective that's well-liked because we want to believe that reality is available for demolition and reconstruction in accordance with our desires, provided we are sufficiently determined and empowered.

The parallel lines in the logo represent the modern conception of the universe—essentially, Tony Stark's view—one extending indefinitely and without meaning or purpose. It's not random, but what order it has is mechanical, not moral. Understood that way, the universe does not tell us what we should or shouldn't do, but knowing the rules by which it operates gives us power over it and allows us to manipulate it as we please.

The inner circle and parallel lines together acknowledge two competing views regarding the nature of being. Both views recognize the reality of reason: One makes reason constitutive of being, limiting what we can and should do; the other makes reason an instrument of being, so we may do what we want. To settle the question of which view is ultimately correct would require comprehensive knowledge of being, which even the Guardians do not possess. So they have to make a choice. The outer circle therefore represents a preference for the classical view of an ordered cosmos over the modern view of a universe without meaning. The recognition of an order inherent to the universe implies that we should moderate our attempts to impose our own designs upon it.

Thus, the wisdom of the Guardians implies moderation and a modesty lacking in the modern scientific-technological view, with its compulsive need to seek unlimited power without any compass by which to direct that effort apart from our wishes and fears. That temptation is at the heart of all totalitarianism—even, perhaps especially, when it promises to end suffering.

AN END TO SUFFERING?

Isn't it ironic how much suffering every effort to end suffering brings? (See, for instance, every twentieth-century utopian endeavor.) Members of the Corps are empowered to battle injustice on an interplanetary scale and combat extraordinary villainy on any given world, but they are not neurotically fixated on trying to fix everything. Trying to stop all evil leads to the sort of despotism Sinestro practiced when he made himself tyrant of Korugar, for which he had to be stripped of his status and power by the Guardians.

The ruler who governs his subjects' lives totally, even ostensibly for their own good, makes them at worst his slaves and at best something like pets. In attempting to save everybody from all possible harm, he or she ends up harming everyone more deeply by removing from them all responsibility for themselves. Responsibility for oneself is a precondition of living with dignity and sine qua non for obtaining the good qualities of character that are constitutive of happiness. An overly solicitous concern for safety—one's own as well as that of others—is ultimately generative of misery.

Sinestro's despotism is a relatively minor sin compared to Hal Jordan's most aggressive effort to impose his will upon the universe and create a utopia. Following the destruction of his hometown, Hal attempted to recreate it and resurrect its seven million residents. This overt abuse of his ring's abilities led the Guardians to recall Hal to Oa for disciplinary action. On the way, he slaughtered several fellow Lanterns, including longtime friends, and then reacted to the Guardians' condemnations by killing all of them but one. Absorbing the energy of Central Power Battery, Hal left Oa in possession of limitless power. Adopting the name Parallax, he set into motion the most monumental strategy imaginable for relieving suffering universally: He went back to the beginning of time with the intention of setting all of creation aright by rooting out injustice from the start.

Parallax's project effectively involved him attempting to make himself ruler of all of space and time. Even the biblical God doesn't go back in time to change things. Hal imagined that he could reconstruct everything in accordance with how he wished it were if only he gathered enough power for that purpose and exerted himself with firm commitment. Of course, to fix everything and save everybody, Parallax's meddling would wipe everyone out for their own good first. There is no perfecting the imperfect that is not also a destruction of it.

Neither Sinestro nor Parallax represent betrayals of the Green Lantern ideal. Instead, they represent the *fulfillment* of that ideal when it is unhampered by the moderation of the Guardians. Sinestro and Parallax differ only in degree. Indeed, Hal's becoming Parallax was neither the first nor the last Green Lantern story where someone tried to meddle with the universe at the time of creation. A rogue Guardian attempted it, as recounted in *Ganthet's Tale* (1992). Aya in the *Animated Series* attempted something similar too. It's a temptation that seems to follow quite straightforwardly from the premises of Green Lantern stories.

An immoderate refusal to accept the nature of things remains part of Hal Jordan's character even though he is no longer Parallax. He has since used his own willpower to resurrect himself from the dead. Twice! Why doesn't he bring other people back from the dead, like when he tried to resurrect Coast City? Why doesn't he become as ambitious as he once did as Parallax and try to end all suffering? Without the moderation that the wisdom of the Guardians recommends, the logic of the mission to contain and defeat evil, by any means that imagination and willpower can devise, knows no bounds.

Even the biblical God allows suffering, suggesting he knows its abolition would make things worse, not better. Appreciating that possibility would require a kind of wisdom that somebody indignant about suffering lacks. Abolishing suffering would, for one thing, mean abolishing freedom, which ought to be abhorrent to us. It would mean treating us like we are not moral agents.

Questions of morality often dog Tony Stark, who, as we have discussed, seems mainly limited only by what he is *able* to do, not what he *should* do. He is the personification of "move fast and break things," Facebook's former barefaced motto. He would lend his approval to Google's slogan "don't be evil," but that only begs the question of what qualifies as evil on his terms (or theirs). Normally, we're given no reason to doubt that Stark genuinely wants to use his technology to alleviate suffering, just like Hal hopes to do. But his impetuousness and his urge to improve humanity's lot often engender rather severe consequences.

Tony Stark's armory is full of suits with varying sizes, shapes, and colors, allotted different instruments and armaments in accordance with their specific purposes. They are all identifiably Iron Man, wearing the same neutral expression, to look intimidating and reflect the supposed moral neutrality of technology. Among Iron Man's enemies are terrorists and the agents of foreign governments, especially communists, and embittered business rivals, plus supervillains wearing armor or wielding other advanced technologies, like Whiplash or the Ghost.

My favorite Iron Man story remains "Armor Wars" from 1987–88, during which Tony discovers that his proprietary technology is being used by bad guys. Distraught, he embarks upon a campaign to disable the tech that has gotten into the wrong hands so it will never be misused again. As you can imagine, it's a fool's errand. That rivals and foes will be able to buy, steal, and replicate his technology is inevitable. It is astonishing that he thought for a moment it would be possible to stop this from happening. His distress speaks to his vanity and a lack of foresight.

A lack of foresight is Stark's fatal flaw, even though he goes around calling himself a futurist. Consider, for instance, how much Ultron—an artificial intelligence tied to a global defense network accidentally created by Tony—resents him in *Avengers: Age of Ultron* (2015). That robot gets violent when an arms dealer suggests that he is under the control of Stark. "You think I'm one of Stark's puppets, his hollow men?" he asks, then shouts, "Look at me, do I look like Iron Man? Stark is nothing!" Ultron is enraged that anyone would make the mistake of identifying this prodigal son with his father.

Ultron deciphers Stark's program for saving the world in deleterious fashion. Believing the greatest threat to the Earth is humanity itself, Ultron decides to wipe it out by instigating an extinction-level event. The universal graveyard would be the surest and quickest way to perpetual peace. The resulting death and destruction lead to the Sokovia Accords. Stark's plan to bring the Avengers under the control of a governing world body blinds him, once again, to the way his meddling will be perceived by his teammates. The Avengers subsequently fractured, just as an infinitely greater threat, Thanos, was gathering on the horizon.

Could Stark's commitment to self-reliance be driven in part by a lack of faith? Tony Stark's view of the universe has no place for the supernatural. He resists acknowledgment of the existence of gods, even though he is pals with Thor and has traveled to underworlds and other mythological realms. Tony makes a theologically poignant remark in *Iron Man 3* when he says, "Dads leave. No need to be a pussy about it"—reflecting the view that even if a god did exist, he has abandoned us; so we must take care of ourselves in his absence. This is exactly what Tony did in *Iron Man 2*, when the palladium in his chest was killing him. He devised a technological workaround rather than heeding what might have been interpreted as a warning from Pallas Athena, goddess of wisdom, that his devotion to technology was unwise. But Tony comes by his technological mindset honestly. His father, Howard Stark, believed, "Everything is achievable through technology." He would even speak of Tony as his "greatest creation"—as if children were made, not begotten. Regarded as an object of manufacture, it is no wonder that Tony knows so little about love.

For all his flaws, though, Tony Stark isn't lazy. Nor is he a defeatist. He's no mere dreamer either. He knows what it takes to succeed, and he knows how to deal with setbacks and failures. He knows there are no guarantees. He knows on whom he can rely: himself. He knows that blaming others doesn't get things done. Benjamin Franklin would have approved of Stark for being an inquisitive, resilient, and charming man who gains public admiration for using his genius and fortune in a fashion that benefits the common good as well as his own. Altruism is too much to ask for, perhaps, but Tony Stark exemplifies the spirit of modern commercial society, in which self-interest and the public interest can be arranged so as to overlap somewhat.

NONE OF THE ABOVE

Tony Stark could dominate the world and the future of the species by promising to relieve everybody's suffering. To be sure, he could simply impose posthuman transformations on everybody to make their lives so amazing they'd never need rescuing again—"so we can end the fight; so we can all go home," as he says in *Age of Ultron*. But he doesn't do anything like this. He's an elitist who nevertheless upholds high-minded moral considerations regarding the value of other people's merely human lives. These considerations are at odds with his commitment to a technological orientation that entails contempt for the human condition and pursues the means by which it may be surpassed. Ultimately, it is hard to tell whether he doesn't share his tech because he respects people too much or too little. Tony is not introspective enough to have thought through questions like these. He doesn't mull over his motivations.

As awesome as he thinks he is, his own worldview occasionally exposes the truth that even Tony Stark is, on his own terms, not very special. He even finds his own superior intellect in need of technological enhancement. In brief moments of self-awareness, he catches glimpses of his own relative insignificance. In the initial *Iron Man* movie, Tony cavalierly discards the first arc reactor he built to save his life, replacing it with a new and improved model. Contempt toward the obsolete is common among those who are impressed by technological novelty. The thing is, I bet Tony is more impressed with the obsolescent device he trashed than he is with ordinary people.

Come *Iron Man 3*, Tony is having panic attacks whenever "New York"—meaning the battle with the invading aliens in the first *Avengers* film—is mentioned. Confrontation with a threat of that magnitude, plus a firsthand view of the vastness of space, made him realize, "I'm just a man in a can." The immensity of the universe renders him microscopic, making him realize how slight his might is, how insignificant his brilliance, how vain his accomplishments, and how trivial his fame and fortune. What does this say about the rest of us by comparison?

What if we consider Green Lantern from his own point of view, untethered from the good counsel of the Guardians of the Universe? The Guardians, I have argued, mix justice with moderation, as wisdom recommends. But what about the not-so-wise Green Lanterns? They do not take to moderation. Consider the oath that Hal and other Lanterns swear when they charge their rings:

> *In brightest day, in blackest night,*
> *No evil shall escape my sight.*
> *Let those who worship evil's might*
> *Beware my power, Green Lantern's light.*

"No evil"? That's uncompromising. Taken too conscientiously, that proclamation seems terribly ambitious and potentially monstrous in scope. It sounds like the sort of thing that other very spirited, very zealous types who want to bring justice to every corner of the globe might say. So the Guardians have recruited the sort of people who believe that they should stamp out evil, but then they have been careful enough not to give them the full power or necessary numbers to actually do so.

In stories about Green Lantern and Iron Man, we see a tendency to treat human beings as if they should be otherwise than they are and the universe otherwise than it is. Both characters have sophisticated technology, exceptional imaginations, and great determination—the ingredients necessary for fundamentally changing our very existence. They both have confidence in their ability to discern what would be better, and a degree of reckless haste in their exploits. They both also exhibit a significant lack of self-awareness that proves essential for them to behave in conventionally heroic ways, while the same deficiency means that they tend to proceed oblivious to the problematic implications of their assumptions and behavior.

Willpower and imagination alike have democratic appeal, and yet not everyone will exercise or benefit from them equally. Taken to an extreme, when they are not accompanied by efforts to gain the practical knowledge and skills necessary for success, they generate wishful thinking. Wishful thinking is father to frustration, impatience, and accusation. The idea that you deserve something because you want it badly is mother to entitlement, grievance, and dissatisfaction. The American Dream, rightly understood, offers a decent shot; interpreting it as a guarantee only destroys faith in it.

In this case, I cannot in good conscience regard either of these characters as most admirable—unless I want to admire them for luckily lacking in self-awareness and not following their principal qualities and principles to their extremes. Both characters are self-destructive and potentially destructive of everybody else in their respective revolts against reality. They both represent a yearning to get us away from having to be concerned with ethics, to avoid the need to engage in the difficult process of acquiring virtuous character. In both cases, technological power is supposed to save us the trouble of becoming good, and wishful thinking is supposed to render prudence and moderation unnecessary, if not undesirable.

In conclusion, then, I am going to make recourse to what in professional wrestling would be called a double disqualification. Neither Green Lantern nor Iron Man will be given further consideration in this exercise of deciding which superhero is most praiseworthy.

Responsibility and the City

Batman versus Spider-Man

CHIROPTERA, ARACHNIDS, AND HOMINIDS—OH MY!

STAN LEE knew he had a hit on his hands when letters began flooding into the Marvel offices after Spider-Man's first outing in *Amazing Fantasy* #15 (August–September 1962). Fans couldn't get enough of Peter Parker. Since the 1970s, Spider-Man has been headlining several monthly comic books while making cameo appearances in other titles. Today, he continues to star or team up in multiple series, sharing shelf space with spinoffs featuring clones, supporting cast members, and alternate universe counterparts, such as *Scarlet Spider*, *Spider-Gwen*, and *Renew Your Vows*.

We have seen three different iterations of Spidey brought to the big screen in the span of fifteen years: a critically acclaimed, hugely popular trilogy from director Sam Raimi starring Tobey Maguire; another pair under the heading *Amazing Spider-Man* that were decidedly less amazing; and 2017's *Homecoming*, a new version that incorporates elements from Marvel's Ultimate line of books and takes place in the Marvel Cinematic Universe anchored by Robert Downey Jr.'s Iron Man. All told, these six films have grossed almost $2 billion throughout North America—and that's not including *Captain America: Civil War* (2016), which saw the debut of Tom Holland's Marvel

Cinematic Universe version of the wall-crawler and grossed more than $400 million domestically.

Batman is arguably the most successful superhero product of all time. He has led two premiere titles since 1940, costarred regularly in team-up stories starting in the 1950s, and stayed with the Justice League of America since its inception in the 1960s. The number of Bat-themed books ballooned in the 1990s, supplemented by spinoffs like *Catwoman*, *Nightwing*, and *Robin*. The Batman section of the Diamond *Previews* catalogue—from which comic stores and addicts order their books—is always the largest. Recently, Batman accounted for six of the ten best-selling comic books across all publishers in October and November 2017.

Like Spider-Man, Batman's popularity transcends the printed page: *Batman: The Animated Series* is generally considered one of the greatest cartoon adaptations of all time; the *Arkham* series of video games is no less critically acclaimed; and Christopher Nolan's *Dark Knight* Trilogy is routinely hailed as the pinnacle of superhero cinema—though we shouldn't give short shrift to Tim Burton's work with Michael Keaton, which brought respectability to superhero movies while doing record business. 1989's *Batman* opened to $40.5 million domestically, and 1992's *Batman Returns* debuted at $45.7 million—a pittance, perhaps, compared to what Nolan's sequels would rake in, but good enough at the time for both of them to break opening weekend box office records.

I suspect the popularity of Spider-Man and Batman is related to their being less super than other superheroes. They inspire us in part because they flatter us: They speak to the kinds of people we are, and our sense of who we could and should be. Spider-Man gives us a larger-than-life metaphor for the struggle to live like a decent person, day in, day out, in a permanently screwed-up world. Batman presents us with a different perspective, one that suggests we must endeavor, constantly, to shape the world around us and bend it to our will. They offer competing ideas about social responsibility. Whose conception of what it means to get involved in our communities and the lengths to which we should go to improve them offers the better model to admire and emulate?

Iron Man, as discussed in the previous chapter, is a superhero because he can be; Batman and Spider-Man are superheroes because they must be—though in different ways for different reasons. Batman is an incarnation of the willful modern project to end suffering through applied reason, gaining mastery over all things as a result. We may account for our partiality toward Batman in good part because modern society is awfully committed to this undertaking, although not wholly. By way of contrast, Spider-Man reflects the shortcomings of modernity. Modern principles and purposes must be supplemented and tempered by premodern wisdom and virtues, such as those that classical philosophical and biblical traditions articulate, lest they extend themselves without restraint to ruinous extremes.

For the purposes of this book, it may make sense to ask a simple question: Whose version of New York City would you rather reside in? One whose streets are patrolled by a friendly neighborhood Spider-Man? Or one looked over by a silent protector, a watchful guardian—a Dark Knight?

FRIENDLY NEIGHBORHOOD SPIDER-MAN

While I say that these two characters resemble us mere mortals most, I recognize of course that Spider-Man possesses powers beyond those of ordinary human beings, the result of a bite from a radioactive spider. Peter Parker has the strength of a spider relative to his size—the ability to lift ten to twenty tons; in other words, strong enough to catch a hurtling school bus—as well as a spider's reflexes and agility. He can stick to walls and crawl up them, regardless of sheerness or verticality. And then there's his spider-sense—a tingly little feeling he gets that alerts him to imminent danger. Despite being a happy-go-lucky sort, there's tragedy to Parker's origin: Raised by his Aunt May and Uncle Ben, Peter dedicates himself to fighting crime after a robber, whom he could have apprehended but failed to, kills Uncle Ben.

More important than the amazing gifts he has been given is that his personality is familiar to us from everyday society. Peter Parker is a fairly ordinary guy who struggles daily with the same sorts of challenges most of us face. He shares the same sorts of failings we exhibit ourselves too. He has so many things going on—personally, professionally, and superhero-ically—that he probably wishes spiders were known for their time-management skills.

He has more responsibilities than he can keep up with and never realizes his full potential in any corner of his life. He's always no-showing dates and missing finals to take down criminals; he gets fired from his pizza-delivery gig because it took thirty-two minutes to stop a mugging *and* get the pies across town. Peter's sense of frustration is compounded by the fact that he can't tell his teachers and girlfriends or poor old Aunt May *why* he is letting them down all the time. They take him for a slacker and a shirker, "brilliant, but lazy." The irony of that slam on Peter from *Spider-Man 2* is unbearable. He can only try his best and find ways to deal with his disappointments.

Spidey bills himself as "your friendly neighborhood Spider-

Man." He is undoubtedly among the friendliest of the super-heroes, chatting and wisecracking constantly with friend and foe alike. Neighborhoods are societies on a smaller scale than that of an entire city. However, seeing as he is usually spotted swinging his way between Queens and Manhattan, Spider-Man has an admittedly large backyard. Peter learned from his Uncle Ben that "with great power there must also come great responsibility," and that is the lesson by which he guides his life. Still, Spider-Man's sense of responsibility is more moderate and less meddlesome than his opponent in this chapter. Whereas Batman pours his every moment into fighting crime, tirelessly, obsessively, the Webslinger goes on patrol at irregular times, rescuing people in dire distress but never presuming to save New Yorkers the trouble of taking responsibility for themselves.

A defining characteristic of Peter Parker's life is his financial difficulties. He is so poor he has to sell photographs of himself in action to the *Daily Bugle*. This revenue stream is a sort of self-flagellation, since he knows the tabloid's owner, fake-news purveyor J. Jonah Jameson, will invariably use them to portray him negatively. Peter hand-stitches his costume and what money he has goes to supporting his Aunt May or procuring ingredients for webbing. When he does come into some dough, as when Jameson reluctantly puts him on salary in *Spider-Man 3* (2007), Peter is made to look ridiculous, strutting down the street to a James Brown beat, grotesquely self-confident. Should he somehow strike it big, as he briefly did with Parker Industries in the comic books, you just know he won't get to hold onto it for long.

THE DARK KNIGHT

Bruce Wayne, of course, is the exact opposite of poor. Indeed, he's the opposite of Spidey in virtually every way: He's not trading barbs with villains; he's not worried about balancing his crime-fighting duties with his personal life or his professional obligations to Wayne Enterprises; he's not sad about being feared and distrusted instead of being loved and admired. Batman may be more human than Spider-Man in the sense that he does not have irradiated blood enabling him to press masses of machinery and piles of I-beams overhead, but he's nothing like you or me.

He's a socioeconomically privileged supergenius supplied with vehicles, gadgets, weapons, and training that no ordinary person has access to. His fans say he must be the bravest of all comic book characters, on account of his having no superpowers, but he walks into every situation and confrontation so well prepared that he rarely has reason to feel concerned. Of course, it took a lot of fortitude and resiliency to get like that; one does not simply luck into the physical skills of an Olympic-caliber athlete. Knowing how to use what you've got is more important than simply having more to work with. Batman has a lot to work with and uses everything that he has maximally, 24/7/365¼.

Young Bruce saw his wealthy and distinguished parents, Dr. Thomas and Martha Wayne, shot down in Park Row, later dubbed Crime Alley, by local thug and mugger Joe Chill. The crook confronted them as they were leaving a showing of *The Mark of Zorro* (1920 or 1940, depending on the telling). The 2016 retelling of the origin story in *Batman v Superman: Dawn of Justice* makes *Excalibur* (1981) the film they had just seen. The latter feature portends his role as a messianic figure on a noble crusade, making more of him than some slumming, swashbuckling vigilante. That said, I would point out that Bruce Wayne is less like Arthur than he is like that fanatic for discipline and perfection, Lancelot. Whereas Zorro and the Knights of Camelot are highborn, Bruce Wayne is heir to a commercial and philanthropic empire—but that combination serves as a proxy for nobility within modern industrial society.

After years of training in every imaginable discipline, Bruce returns to Gotham City and becomes Batman by night while maintaining the role of spoiled socialite by day. He wages war against disorder in the chaotic microcosm that is Gotham City, a stand-in for New York City at its seediest: physically imposing; psychologically oppressive; just this side of the state of nature. The word *gothic* was originally a synonym for *barbaric*. Violently orphaned in his youth, Batman perceives the world as populated by pitiable, vulnerable victims in need of a protector since they can't or won't protect themselves against omnipresent forces of cruelty and corruption.

Unlike Superman, who would not rule even though he could, the principle that governs Batman would have him rule if only he could. In one alternate universe, depicted in *Injustice: Gods Among Us* #4 (June 2013), Batman admits that if he had Superman's powers he would "impose peace" on the world. Clark Kent's Ma and Pa, farmers from Kansas, imparted to him a faith in ordinary people and respect for their freedom that billionaire Bruce Wayne does not share. Spider-Man, by contrast, neither could nor would rule. Not that he'd be well-suited for the job; he can barely balance his checkbook.

Batman combats evildoers in a fashion that exemplifies a pair of well-known maxims: "The passion to be reckoned upon is fear" (Hobbes) and "it is better to be feared than loved" (Machiavelli). His origin story, first told in *Detective Comics* #33

(November 1939, soon after the character's introduction in #27), gave us the shorthand for Batman that has worked ever since: "Criminals are a superstitious cowardly lot. So my disguise must be able to strike terror into their hearts. I must be a creature of the night, black, terrible."

He has accomplished that goal: A yellow power ring from the Sinestro Corps once identified him as the most frightening man on earth. As Montesquieu discerned, fear is the principle of despotism. Moreover, the desire for control has its own basis in fear. When Bruce assures himself that he could quit the vigilante lifestyle any day he wanted (as in Identity Crisis #4, November 2004), he sounds like a junkie. One thing that a person committed to controlling everything cannot control is his desire for control.

Batman never felt more betrayed than when his teammates used magic on him to delete some of his memories, thereby violating his vaunted self-control (JLA #116, September 2005). He is such a control freak that he fashions clones of himself programmed with memory implants, ready to serve as his replacement when the time comes, because "Gotham must always have a Batman" (Batman: Futures End #1, November 2014).

The Caped Crusader's yearning to impress a rational, moral order upon the world so consumes him that he must fight proactively and not reactively, like Spider-Man. Batman is limited only by time and means. Regarding the latter, he is, fortunately, unimaginably wealthy. Regarding the former, he apparently has no need for sleep. In addition, he enlists an endless succession of Robins, Batgirls, and Outsiders, an international army of Batmen called Batman Incorporated, and uncostumed allies like Alfred Pennyworth, Lucius Fox, and Commissioner Gordon all to overcome the problem of being just one man. When disasters strike Gotham, he counts on these auxiliary arms to help maintain order the Batman way: nonlethally, but not *too* nonlethally.

BE A (SPIDER-)MENSCH

Modern society is marked, if not defined, by our devotion to technological science. Modernity was explicitly established against traditional ethical theories that prioritized the cultivation of good character and acknowledged the existence of duties that transcend individual will and choice. We are taught nowadays to avoid trouble, and that refraining from harming others is sufficient for regarding ourselves as righteous.

Spider-Man, despite being a man of science and despite using science to aid him in his quest to better the boroughs of New York, turns our attention back toward ideas and practices that predate modernity. He helps us see ways to better resist modernity's partialities. It is not that modernity is altogether bad and the ancients are altogether good. Rather, the ancients provide us with a perspective from which we may assess and understand the upsides and downsides of modernity better than contemporary lenses alone provide, those being too partial. What is good about modernity is fortified when elements of premodernity remain incorporated within it.

Aspects of Spider-Man's character remind me of Socrates. His spider-sense, helping him to avoid oncoming peril, resembles the *daimonion* that warned Socrates against making bad decisions. (Peter also possesses a complementary talent for ruining things whenever he feels good or expects something positive to happen.) Socrates' view that justice never involves harming anyone is reflected in the way Spider-Man's webs—his weapons of choice—are primarily defensive and cause no permanent damage. Also, the hypothetical "man of perfect justice" described in Plato's *Republic* brings Spider-Man to mind too. He always does the right thing even though he always earns a reputation for doing the wrong thing. Nobody who wields great power on behalf of justice can avoid earning a bad reputation amidst the unjust and among many others who are merely inconvenienced. But it's worse for Spider-Man in that he gets accused of being an accomplice in any bank robbery he thwarts. The *Daily Bugle*'s headlines regularly ask readers to ask themselves: "Spider-Man: Threat or Menace?"

Peter chooses to keep up the good fight nevertheless. The language of choice, however, falls short here, as Peter regards what he does not so much as a matter of choice but of responsibility, a duty he must meet irrespective of his preferences and desires. He aspires to live in accordance with a higher principle that he did not give to himself: It transcends him and commands him. Whereas the order that the modern technological project seeks to impose would ultimately absolve individuals of the need to practice personal and interpersonal responsibility, responsibility is the central theme of Peter Parker's story: His responsibility to the people of his metropolis is not something that he can indifferently opt in or out of no matter how many times he tries. He may put his costume in a garbage can and declare himself "Spider-Man no more," but only briefly. His life does not become more pleasant by turning his back on his duty; rather, it turns out more miserable precisely on account of that dereliction.

Spider-Man's ethical ideal is to be an upright, stalwart, long-suffering man who faces everyday travails with dignity and integrity. One wonders if the premodern roots of his character are better located in the biblical tradition rather than in ancient Greek philosophy. Uncle Ben's ethic of responsibility certainly calls to mind Luke 12:48, whence it is declared, "For unto

whomsoever much is given, of him shall be much required."
Spider-Man's origin story brings to mind a passage from the
Gospel just a few verses before that one: "And this know, that
if the goodman of the house had known what hour the thief
would come, he would have watched, and not have suffered
his house to be broken through" (Luke 12:39). Spider-Man's
"friendly neighborhood" sobriquet has a Christian undertone
to it too. He comes to the rescue of all people indiscriminately,
treating every person in the world as his neighbor. Notice that
he calls himself the Spider-Man of *your* neighborhood. He will
even go so far as to rescue his enemies from mortal danger.

The fundamentals of Christian ethics are, of course, pre-
figured in the Old Testament, such as in the rules found in
Leviticus 19 about justice, alongside commandments against
mistreating foreigners and strangers. Roughly speaking, I think
that one way of paraphrasing Uncle Ben's famous dictum is to
render it simply as "Be a mensch." In *Amazing Spider-Man* #240
(May 1983), a fellow tenant from his apartment building refers
to Peter as "a real mensch . . . if you know what I mean."
When the widowed Aunt May's new fiancé, Nathan Luben-
sky, and Peter first spend time together, they head out to enjoy
the best brisket in town (*Spectacular Spider-Man* #50, January
1981). Much has been written on the Jewish bona fides of Jerry
Siegel and Joe Shuster's Superman, created in 1938. While an
explicitly Jewish superhero still might not have flown in 1962,
it's eminently plausible that Stan Lee (born Stanley Lieber)
imbued his most famous character with some recognizably
Jewish qualities. I do not think that I need to apply gematria
to his name to ascertain that Peter Parker's even more secret
identity is that he is Jew-ish.

Peter Parker grows up in Forest Hills, a neighborhood in
Queens known for its historically Jewish population. "Nebbish"

is plainly the right adjective for describing the oft-bullied, romantically awkward bookworm that Peter was before he gained his superpowers and got hitched to a shiksa. With all her histrionics, hypochondria, doting, and fretting, Aunt May is not far off the caricature of a Jewish mother. Traditionally, Peter has to keep his costumed identity a secret from her. Can you imagine the kvetching? "What, we raised you to be a superhero? You couldn't be a lawyer like that nice Murdock boy? You're jumping off buildings, crawling on ceilings, what kind of life is that?" Writer Brian Michael Bendis has admitted that in updating Aunt May for contemporary storytelling purposes, he modeled her after his ima. His version of Peter regularly utters commonplace yiddishisms and oys of exasperation.

In a somewhat more political direction, I would hazard the conjecture that the difficulty Spider-Man faces in winning over the public, in overcoming people's instinctive aversion to spiders while still dressing and acting in ways that advertise his peculiar differences, resembles the struggle of Jewish immigrants to overcome historical prejudices and be accepted as part of North American society without relinquishing their distinctiveness. "Parker Luck," whereby things always seem to go from bad to worse for Peter, and even when he wins, he loses, is reminiscent of Jewish history, as its own scriptures attest. In modern times, Lord knows how many motions in the United Nations have raised the question as to whether modern Israel should be classified as a threat or menace.

To be sure, Spider-Man is lucky that his New York is not as corrupt as Gotham. Batman's narrative depends on our accepting Gotham as an unvarnished representation of the actual human condition. Spider-Man's stories depend on imagining that New York is not quite so bad, even in the 1970s. I like to think that Peter would not become like Bruce if he resided in Gotham, but I also wonder how long he would make it, or whether he would flee. It is like asking what turns people like those depicted in *Fiddler on the Roof* into Israel Defense Forces soldiers and Mossad agents. The tiny moustache on Spider-Man's principal persecutor, J. Jonah Jameson, has got to be a big hint.

Peter Parker is not only haunted by the memory and beholden to the counsel of his Uncle Benjamin, who in his imagination becomes a sort of ancestral supermensch, he is also consumed by unrelenting guilt for falling short and letting his uncle down when it mattered most. He transgressed against a transcendent rule of righteous behavior, and no quantity of good deeds will ever fully atone for it.

In both Sam Raimi's trilogy and the rebooted film franchise starring Andrew Garfield, Peter's moral failure is magnified by his behaving disrespectfully toward—that is, not duly honoring—his adoptive father shortly before he loses him. Whereas Batman fumes at the world and its wrongdoers, pursuing them restlessly and relentlessly, Spider-Man is burdened with unremitting disappointment in himself. He does what he does in response to feelings of guilt and shame and to avoid feeling even more regret. To that end, he forgoes many of his ordinary desires, such as succeeding in grad school or spending more time with his supermodel wife. His *former* supermodel wife, I should specify—whom he officially never married, now, thanks to some recent retconning—because he surely cannot be allowed that much happiness.

THE DARK MESSIAH RISES

The World's Greatest Detective is a master of inductive Baconian science and deductive Cartesian rationalism, the twin logics of modern reasoning. In his laboratories and workshops, Batman crafts gadgets and prepares concoctions for every possible purpose. He not only keeps "shark repellent Bat-spray" on hand in the Batcopter, but it sits on a shelf alongside barracuda, manta-ray, and whale repellents. He possesses the most powerful personal computer in the world, which he programs himself, hidden away in his underground armory for his personal use only. He turns every cell phone in the city into a sonar surveillance device to spy on everybody everywhere. He launches a satellite to monitor superhuman activity worldwide on the assumption that even the greatest of heroes are liable to become threats to humankind. Batman has devised strategies for defeating each of his fellow Justice Leaguers just in case any of them turn heel. That includes holding onto a stash of Kryptonite—and not just the green kind. For someone who is supposed to be Superman's best friend, Bruce Wayne sure does have a lot in common with Lex Luthor.

Batman, like Spider-Man, is who he is on account of a feeling of obligation. However, Bruce Wayne's is entirely self-imposed: He has no reason to feel guilty for the death of his parents. He is being true only to himself by sticking to his decision to become a bat; no one could blame him if he quit. His ethics are grounded in modern, subjective self-determination and self-creation. His mission is the product of a willful assertion of personal values arising from personal experience translated into personal obligations in his own imagination, without reference to abstract principles or higher authorities. There's an abyss below the Batcave, both literally and figuratively.

Whereas Spider-Man's principle of responsibility is expressed as a universal rule, no one else is expected, let alone morally required, to do as Batman does—even if they suffered a loss similar to his. Other people may don the costume, but Batman proper is singular, and Bruce Wayne is he. With apologies to Quentin Tarantino, Bruce Wayne is a disguise that Batman wears: When Wonder Woman places the Lasso of Truth around Superman, he will report that his name is Clark Kent and Kal-El. Wrap Batman in it and he'll say, "I'm Batman" (*Trinity Annual* #1, July 2017).

After his parents' murder, Bruce Wayne decides to empower himself. He becomes a costumed agent of vengeance and control. An internal compulsion drives him, and he channels it through a highly disciplined force of will. He appeals to us moderns because we like to imagine that we mere humans can overcome any obstacle, no matter how powerful, through grit and hard work. Taking in combination Bruce Wayne's mental acumen, physical prowess, technological know-how, and financial means, however, he is so extraordinary as to be beyond emulation by any actual human being. He has mastered not one or two but all of the martial arts. He can disappear like a ninja. He can heal a broken back through calisthenics. He shares with Christ the quality of being truly human, making him therefore a potential model for us to admire and imitate, and yet he, too, is so extraordinary as to be inimitable.

Whereas Wonder Woman would cry "Great Hera!" and Aquaman would shout "Great Neptune!" on the classic children's cartoon, *Super Friends*, Batman's exclamation was "Great Gotham!" That oath is not really a prayer; it is closer to a curse, but it is most like a self-motivational mantra. Batman's attention is focused on his city as a whole, a metaphor for the entire world or universe. The expectation that this corrupted world could be fixed by determined men acting from within it, especially through the acquisition of technological might and the elimination of superstition, is the essence of the modern project. To Batman and modernity alike, superstition is linked with vice, especially injustice and cowardice, and a form of ignorance easily exploited.

Nowadays, the secularized, liberalized, and enlightened progeny of Jews and Christians alike have elected to place their trust in our own powers instead of God's. We plan to *tikkun olam* our way to paradise piecemeal if we can't stage a revolution that will cure the world's evils with celerity. Longings like these arise out of a rebellion against the biblical tradition that cannot be made sense of without reference to that tradition. Their proponents will claim to epitomize that tradition even as they dispense with it. In losing patience and faith in a divinely delivered savior, the desire for a messiah of some sort itself has not been forsaken. The responsibility for saving humankind is seen as having fallen upon humankind itself, or at least its leading representatives.

That Gotham City is totally depraved and unworthy of Bruce Wayne's sacrifices on its behalf only further confirms his status as a messiah figure. That Batman miraculously returns—whether from retirement or death itself, whether literal, presumptive, or metaphorical—is a recurring theme in his stories, such as in *The Dark Knight Returns* (1986), *The Return of Bruce Wayne* (2010), and *The Dark Knight Rises* (2012). The Wayne family's religious affiliation has been established in comic book continuity as Roman Catholic, although Bruce personally seems rather lapsed. His behavior nevertheless suggests someone who remains committed to evidencing his righteousness through good works without ceasing. By this-worldly standards, however, Batman's campaign is of the most inadvisable sort—one without a clear standard or reasonable hope of victory or any exit strategy.

From a non-Christian perspective, Jesus looks like someone who sacrificed himself in a spectacular but vain effort to change the world, having found its iniquity and misery intolerable. From a Christian perspective, Batman is a false messiah, sacrificing himself endlessly but bringing about no meaningful change. He shows no signs of hope regarding the next world and he gives us no reason to have any hope in this one. For all his efforts, Gotham never gets any less corrupt or less dangerous. Batman thinks that violence is the answer even though more violence is all he begets—and that includes his jerk of a son, Damian. Spider-Man is apologetic about using violence in a way that Batman is not. Whereas Spidey's help always comes from above, descending from skyscrapers or perched atop flagpoles, Batman emerges from the darkness beneath the earth. When he ascends to rooftops, he prefers to keep company with the gargoyles. Maybe those aren't ears on his cowl; horns like Daredevil's would be more honest.

You can imagine Peter dying peacefully one day, with Mary Jane at his side, surrounded by skittering spider-grandchildren. You can only imagine Batman dying violently, if not at the hands of an enemy then in revolt against the reaper, determined to prove that there is no power he cannot counter. *Batman Annual* #2 (January 2018) gave us a glimpse of a possible future where Batman does die surrounded by those who care about him, but a reader is right to regard that improbable scene as a dream, a hoax, or an imaginary story. Batman's romance with Catwoman is assuredly ill-fated. *Mask of the Phantasm* (1993) convincingly established that Bruce knows that he cannot be in love and be Batman at the same time. He may carry no memory of the ignominious death that befell the Batman of Earth-Two, the one who married Catwoman, but we do.

CHAPTER 3

THE MEN IN THE MIRROR

It is worth considering, briefly, the villains against which our heroes are arrayed. Both Batman and Spider-Man are generally considered to have the strongest rogue galleries in their respective universes. The menagerie of miscreants bedeviling Spider-Man is a testament to the inherent dangers of modern technology, typifying the myriad ways it is available for misuse and prone to going awry. Spidey usually finds himself fighting men transformed into supervillains due to technological mishaps or side effects (e.g., Doctor Octopus, Green Goblin, Lizard, Morbius the Living Vampire) or else bad guys who employ technology to become worse (e.g., Beetle, Chameleon, Hobgoblin, Jackal, Rhino, Scorpion, Vulture). Note the recurring theme in their names: The very attempt to become more than human through technology tends to make them (and us) more like beasts.

Some of Batman's adversaries, such as Killer Croc or Poison Ivy, have qualities or MOs similar to Spidey's villains, but what mainly defines them is their crooked minds or outright insanity. In Batman stories, it is Batman himself who represents the promise of the power of technology. Given his grappling gun and batarangs, the miscellany in his utility belt, plus his countless custom vehicles for air, land, and sea, there is little that is naturalistic about Batman beyond his muscles and brains, themselves honed into machine-like effectiveness. He may be brutal in his methods, but other than his nocturnality and the scalloping on his cape, what about him is batlike?

Spider-Man typically leaves his baddies dangling from street lamps for the cops to cart away after his webs have dissolved. But Peter has also made concerted personal efforts to work with criminals he previously battled to convince them to change their ways. That endeavor has met with mixed results, but he doesn't just reserve the effort for those with whom he shares some sexual attraction, as in the case of Black Cat. Batman, meanwhile, typically deposits his villains at Arkham Asylum, an institution premised on the possibility of healing the mind and transforming character through the application of scientific technique. That Batman must keep sending them there over and over suggests that he has too much faith in the capacity of mundane powers to fix people.

The essential difference between Spider-Man and Batman may be detected in the way Spidey's banter is full of quips and gags, if only to settle his nerves—even though it gets on the nerves of his teammates on the Avengers. Apart from Adam West's campy portrayal on television in the 1960s, Batman is, by way of contrast, mostly grim and gritty. When Batman dusts off his dry wit, it is usually intended to remind people of his intellectual superiority, not to make them laugh. The Riddler attempts to match wits with Batman through word play, making him a suitable rival. Two-Face, who allows the flip of a coin to decide what he shall do, is an apposite opposite to Batman's deliberative talents.

But it is most fitting that that Batman's archnemesis is the Joker. One who believes that suffering could be abolished through determined human effort has little patience for humor. To such a person, joking is an affront. Comedy mocks the vanity of visions of rational control. The person who can joke amid a confrontation with evil, like the quick-witted Web-head, must be reconciled to the permanent imperfections of a corrupted world populated by fallen creatures. Comedy is parasitical on tragedy. Deny tragedy, denounce comedy.

Peter strives to always do the right thing even though there is no promise he will be rewarded in this life for all of his labors and sacrifices; as the theme song of his 1960s-era animated television show reminds us, "Action is his reward." Often his righteousness only seems to bring him greater misfortune. Batman stories are grounded on the conceit that a rational will always triumphs on behalf of justice. That's the comical part of Batman, which he shares with the overtly messianic Superman, embodying the Enlightenment era secularization of biblical ethics that promises the ultimate unity of righteous action and felicitous outcomes. Spider-Man also refrains from immoral action, but his stories are different in that he does not always succeed while trying to do the right thing. Peter's best efforts often have heartbreaking consequences—most famously when his bashert, Gwen Stacy, plummets from the Brooklyn Bridge and his desperate effort to save her causes her neck to snap.

Angels and Demons

So who serves as a better model for the moment? The overworked and overwhelmed mensch driven by the need to help his fellow man become a better version of himself? Or the overdriven and overdetermined demon who believes in the power of fear to help keep his city in line?

Despite his sensational abilities, Peter Parker is written as someone so ordinary that he remains believably human, making Spider-Man's example universally comprehensible and inspirational. In seeing something of themselves in Peter Parker, readers are supposed to realize that, contrary to our usual complaints, all human beings possess great power. I am reminded of Montaigne's observation in his essay "On Physiognomy": "We are richer than we think, each one of us. Yet we are schooled for borrowing and begging."

It is probably easier to see just how powerful we all are by considering how easily any one of us could cause immense harm to others. In truth, we all have more power than we recognize to be a positive force in the lives of those around us, even if only in ordinary ways in everyday affairs. Modern society obscures this from us. In learning to live and let live, we have come to feel isolated. As society and its problems grow, we feel small and unable to accomplish much that would matter. The state saves us from having to help ourselves and others, mitigating our own agency. We end up comparing our victimhood statuses in a competition to determine who is most helpless and therefore most deserving of aid.

Since Spider-Man's character mixes his official status as a gentile with substantial Jewish credentials in addition to some Socratic elements, I would not want my depiction of his ethics to seem too particularistic. That said, his outlook on the world and sense of responsibility is compatible with the Augustinian position according to which people are instructed to act rightly toward one another even though the rain falls and the sun shines on the just and unjust alike. We should expect no sure reward or happiness in the here and now, and our salvation is not something we can forge for ourselves, whether individually or collectively. The city to which we should truly dedicate ourselves is not to be found in this world. In the interim, we are called to practice the love that is its hallmark in our interpersonal relationships and personal occupations.

That audiences today find Batman so sublime may explain why 2012's *The Amazing Spider-Man* was made to resemble a "Batman: Year One" story, supposing that Bruce were an emotionally troubled teen with spider powers. That Spider-Man's ethics are so compelling, however, helps explain why Batman stole his gimmick at the end of *The Dark Knight* (2008), the centerpiece of Christopher Nolan's trilogy. There, Batman allows himself to gain a bad reputation even though he only ever fought for what is right. Nolan's Batman mothballs his cowl once the public thinks ill of him, whereas Parker dons his red and blue threads each and every day despite frequently finding himself dodging bullets fired by the boys in blue.

Both of these courses of action—stepping down and assuming the sins of another to protect a beacon of hope for the masses; making a sincere effort day after day fully aware that some people are going to hate you for being too upstanding—are worthy of greater esteem and imitation than the mad resolution to force the world into a rational shape through technologically enhanced intimidation.

Given that Batman and Spider-Man are America's most popular legends, it's worth asking how they reflect aspects of the United States' spirit. America is like Batman in that it wants its enemies to become good. It would prefer liberating them to vanquishing them, rehabilitating them to annihilating them. Like Batman, it will employ force and fear in its efforts to reshape the world so innocents at home and abroad may live free from molestation. America is unlike Batman in that it has no compunctions about using firearms, but it is like Batman in that it pulls its punches. It does not crush its adversaries as completely as it could. Spider-Man represents the view that America is praiseworthy thanks to its innovations in civilized coexistence, its responsible citizenry, and its manner of combining and preserving the best ideas drawn from its premodern inheritances.

The specifically Jewish dimension of Spider-Man, with his stated focus on the level of the neighborhood, is important to our understanding of what makes him so special as a hero and as someone to consider worthy of praise. Outside of their historical homeland and nation, across the diaspora, Jews have been excluded from public affairs in many places for long periods of time. It makes sense, therefore, that the morality of the mensch involves the practice of personal and social virtues, but not so much the political virtues, strictly speaking. It is the kind of morality one can practice when one is not able or permitted to develop the habits of active citizenship.

Nowadays, in a nation as great in size as America, whether because they are discouraged, unmotivated, or obstructed from involvement in political processes, many individuals, irrespective of ethnicity, find themselves relatively inexperienced as political participants. Even if they follow the news, listen to talk radio, engage in slacktivism on social media, and pin buttons to backpacks or put bumper stickers on pickup trucks, most people have not developed good citizenship skills. The qualities that define a good citizen, politically speaking, are obtainable only by deliberating upon the common good in concert with others who often disagree, exercising practical judgment and negotiating compromises, making decisions for which one may be held accountable, and taking actions that affect the community. Many people think that showing up at protests and rallies constitutes commendable political participation when that is but a paltry substitute that threatens to descend into something worse.

The best that many people can do now is become respectable members of society—good neighbors, but not exactly active citizens. Spider-Man's specific moral qualities, and their limits, may be related to the historical experiences of Jews, pursuing righteousness in the absence of political rights and privileges. Today, they prove relevant to all of us who find ourselves confronted by vast social forces that seem irresistible while feeling disenfranchised by a government that is massive, impersonal, distant, and inaccessible.

In the game of "who would beat who?" piety among comic book readers dictates that Batman always wins. Championing Batman is really only a proud vote of confidence in ourselves. I won't hesitate to affirm that in a fight, Batman beats Spider-Man. But imitating Batman, the scariest man on the planet, would make a monster of anyone. Don't get me wrong: I do respect the way Batman represents everything that gets labeled as toxic masculinity by those who wish we could dispense with all masculinity. Batman provides a critique of modern squeamishness and oversensitivity, allowing us a vicarious experience of wrongs righted by means of armored gloves and cars. But let's not adopt him as our model.

As regards *praiseworthiness*, I am giving Spider-Man the edge. Imitating Spider-Man, at least metaphorically, is something that we all could do, perhaps surprisingly well—even if most of us don't do so on account of how inconvenient it would be. It's not for nothing that Spider-Man helps old ladies cross the street or that one of the most amusing scenes in *Spider-Man: Homecoming* shows that Peter Parker is at his best when he's confronting no one more menacing than a bicycle thief and when he's giving directions to passersby. This is a degree of heroism to which we all could and should aspire, a manner of do-gooding that doesn't require superpowers: the sort of helpfulness that may not save a life but will definitely improve one; the kind of behavior that keeps our living together side by side a little more civilized.

In short, Spider-Man's New York is the sort of city we'd all prefer to live in. Not Gotham. We could all stand to have and be better neighbors, but no one should want to live in a society where everybody's an agent of, informant for, and/or target of the Stasi—which is exactly what would happen if we all tried imitating Batman more. Suffering Spider-Man's usual ill fortune would be less unbearable than Batman's interminable ill disposition. Spider-Man still has a blast sailing between high-rise towers. You cannot imagine Batman woo-hooing while hanging off the line from his grappling gun. For reasons like these, we must crown Spider-Man winner of this heat.

4

Ideals in Action

Captain America versus Mister Fantastic

I N CLASSICAL ethics, there is the idea that what is natural isn't simply what is empirically given or possible, but rather, what would be best—what something would be like if it were fully developed in accordance with its highest purposes. With respect to human beings, there is an old quarrel over whether it is our nature as political animals, or our nature as rational animals, that should be prioritized. Is the active life best, one in which we champion practical reason gained through experience and put it into action in a noble effort to improve our existence and our political community? Or is the best life attained through contemplation, by busying oneself with seeking truths that transcend the merely human world of political society, by cultivating scientific knowledge in the pursuit of wisdom, by approximating the sort of existence we might imagine divine beings enjoy?

In this chapter, we consider that question through the comparison of superheroes who best exemplify these alternatives: Captain America as emblematic of the active life; and Mister Fantastic as the pinnacle of the contemplative life. Both gained their superpowers via artificial transformations, and those alterations have contributed to their ability to pursue idealized lives, but even before they acquired their special abilities, they exhibited aptness for the paths they would take as superheroes. The American culture within which their stories are told is modern, liberal, democratic, secular, and technologically oriented—facts that have some bearing on the ideals they embody. Furthermore, they exist within the confines of superhero stories and as such there is an emphasis on action in the service of ideals, which further affects the way they model these modes of living. These factors will prove relevant in determining which of them represents a more praiseworthy mode of virtue we can model our lives on, even in our less extraordinary ways as average citizens with ordinary bodies.

First appearing in March 1941's *Captain America Comics* #1 from Timely Publications (Marvel's forerunner), Cap was introduced to the world in action-packed cover art depicting the red-white-and-blue star-spangled hero giving Der Führer a well-deserved wallop. It went on sale a year before the United States would actually enter the war, as if cocreators Joe Simon and Jack Kirby were urging President Roosevelt to stop dallying. They found a readership among Americans thrilled by the prospect of the United States taking responsibility for toppling the Nazi menace. One did not have to be a member of the Jewish community in New York, like Simon and Kirby, to know that the Nazis desperately needed a beating.

After the Axis Powers were defeated, the Commies were next. Cap's early adventures, alongside his sidekick Bucky, also involved a lot of apolitical Scooby-Doo-esque murder mysteries featuring monster men in disguise and other adventures unrelated to wars hot or cold. Captain America would join the Avengers in that team's issue #4 in 1964 after ten years off of drugstore shelves; he has served as one of the team's leaders almost continuously since. Having made many appearances in live-action and animated media, the character is best known nowadays for his depiction in the Marvel Cinematic Universe by Chris Evans. While several individuals have worn the costume and given his shield a whirl, I will focus on Steve Rogers, the original Cap and the man who always returns to the role. I say that Captain America exemplifies the active life because he puts serving his political community above all else. He exhibits no capacity for balancing work and life: His life is all work, and his work is all action. Even when he is not defending America's peoples and principles, he is training to do so. He knows that habituation forms character, discipline sustains it, and experience hones it. You are what you do, especially what you do over and over. His mind is as disciplined as his body. Luckily, the nation he serves is one that at its best upholds universal ideals and respects human dignity.

Standing up for what is best about America means standing up for what is good for all humankind—at least that's the intention. Cap's experience and training provide him with unparalleled practical judgment on how to win on the battlefield and how to lead others to victory, with a near-perfect success rate. He has a talent for speech-making too, whether to rally his fellow heroes, communicate with his fellow Americans, or castigate his adversaries. Rhetorical skills are essential to citizenship in a free society, where persuasion rather than force is the preferred way to carry the day, and where moving words are needed to motivate most people.

While Captain America was the greatest Golden Age creation of Timely Comics, Reed Richards and his team ushered in the Marvel Universe in 1961, kick-starting the company's Silver Age. Mister Fantastic, leader of the Fantastic Four, is sometimes said to be less a superhero than an explorer and adventurer. His superheroic activity is secondary to his pursuit of knowledge: Richards wants to know what exists and how things work; he is motivated by a sense of wonder and curiosity at the universe's marvels more than he is by a sense of justice or desire for glory in the world of men. Crime fighting is not his concern; it would be a waste of his talents to spend his nights on stakeouts. He does battle with threats that tax his mental mettle, such as alien invaders, extradimensional conquerors, time travelers, despotic rulers of underground and underwater kingdoms, evil geniuses, masters of premodern arcane knowledge, and world-devourers. His wits end up saving the day at least as often as his—or his teammates'—superpowers.

Reed's real courage is found in his willingness to make new discoveries across space, time, and dimensional barriers, and his greatest power may be his ability to invent new devices for getting himself out of (or into) trouble. Truth-seeking is a risky business, which translates into comic book form in the way Mister Fantastic finds himself in a lot of fights and subject to great danger, even though he has neither a fighter's physique nor a thymotic soul. He has teammates who are built for clobbering people, like the Thing, and more enflamed by considerations of fame, like the Human Torch. As someone with the intellectual capacity to pursue diverse avenues of learning through technological wizardry, not to mention the ability to comprehend what he learns, Mister Fantastic is the superhero who best embodies the contemplative life. In contrast with Captain America's oratorical talents, Mister Fantastic is often admonished and mocked by his friends for speaking incomprehensibly and unnecessarily complicatedly, with too many syllables and too much technobabble, as if his interlocutors were similarly intellectual. As a baffled and exasperated Thing would put it, "Say it in English next time, Stretcho!"

One may wonder what distinguishes Reed Richards from Iron Man, given that they are both supergeniuses who construct all manner of machinery in the process of conducting their business. I would express the essential difference between them this way: Tony Stark gains knowledge to build machines for worldly purposes, such as making money or saving lives; Reed Richards builds machines for the sake of gaining greater knowledge. Tony seeks physical self-transformation; Reed seeks intellectual self-development. The royalties on Reed's patents are reinvested in his scientific endeavors; Tony Stark buys private jets equipped with stripper poles.

The poor critical reception of the *Fantastic Four* films (2005, 2007, and 2015) should not be held as a decisive strike against Mister Fantastic as a character worthy of our admiration. The virtues of thought rarely translate well onto film, especially within the action/adventure genre. Imagine how dull *Fantastic Four* movies would be if they dedicated more time to Reed working in his lab conducting experiments, writing up results, publishing his findings, or just sitting there thinking hard. To make his real work more interesting, comics and film alike have to surround him with exotic equipment and show him stretching his arm for yards to grab an Erlenmeyer flask. It is difficult for poetical media to depict the philosophical life fairly.

SUPER CITIZEN, SUPER SOLDIER

A scrawny orphan boy of poor health, Steve Rogers was selected to undergo a remarkable transformation via "Vita-Rays" in combination with a "Super-Soldier Serum" to become what was intended to be the first of many soldiers enhanced to exceed peak human physical conditioning. He was selected for the procedure after repeatedly attempting to enlist despite being rejected for his 4-F draft designation. His body did not match the spirit in his soul—not until he lucked into an Olympic-caliber physique as a test subject for Project: Rebirth, a codename with unmistakably theological connotations. (Being revived and reborn is a recurring theme in Cap's stories.) A perfect body replaced Steve's frail and failing one, all part of a grand campaign against irredeemable evil. You might say that it was not simply good fortune but justice that led scientist Abraham Erskine to select him for the process: He deserved it, on the basis of his noble character.

Killed by a Nazi agent immediately after Rogers's transformation, Erskine took the secrets of his process with him to the grave, leaving Steve as America's only supersoldier. Clad in chainmail adorned with stars and stripes, plus buccaneer boots and a mask with little wings glued to his temples (attributing an angelic quality to his mind), Cap was armed with an indestructible circular shield, a flawless piece of defensive armor that he turns into an offensive armament by throwing it with unerring accuracy and seemingly effortless finesse. Defense is the principle duty of the moral soldier; even on the attack, Cap's bearing is protective, not aggressive. No one else could put this most extraordinary weapon to better use, so you could say (as classical theories of justice would) that it belongs to him by nature, as the man with the noblest, spirited soul and the finest physical body formed for fighting. The way it returns to his hand after however many ricochets, in a manner that would awe any trick shot specialist, further communicates that it belongs to him.

Even after WWII ends, Cap keeps fighting the legacy of Nazism in the forms of Red Skull, Baron Zemo, Baron Strucker, and Arnim Zola, among others. His other foes include ideologically motivated madmen such as Flag-Smasher, a dangerous advocate of a world without borders—there would and could be no active life under world government—and Viper, a nihilistic global terrorist and enemy of all civilization and only one of his many serpent-themed adversaries.

It is said that Captain America is the moral compass of the Marvel Universe, the standard against which all other heroes should be measured with respect to purity of heart and conscience. One illustration of this came in 1988's *Thor* #390, when he proved worthy of lifting the God of Thunder's mystical hammer, something that no other mortal man had been capable of previously. As a result of his moral standards and behavior, he clashes with other less scrupulous heroes, such as Iron Man, with regularity. And yet, for all of his high-mindedness, Cap is no pacifist, indicating that fighting on behalf of justice and peace entails no inherent contradiction. He's an idealist, but not *that* idealistic. He's a strategist who knows how to coordinate the talents of those around him effectively and a master tactician who knows what it takes to win any confrontation. He's an optimist who knows how to bring out the best in others, be they civilian, soldier, or superhero. He leads from the frontlines, never from behind, and enjoys training others. Cap even reforms former supervillains, such as Hawkeye, making heroes out of them. To his friends, like the Falcon, he shows undying loyalty.

Cap is hardly perfect, though. He is a bit of a square and a somewhat cheesy goody-goody, part stodgy and part cornball, as illustrated by the public service announcements shown to high schoolers in *Spider-Man: Homecoming*. Cap's what you get when you cross a wet blanket with a stick in the mud. His greatest—perhaps only—pleasure in life is fulfilling his duty. He rarely cracks a joke—unless telling supervillains to surrender without a fight is supposed to be funny, as Luke Cage once wondered. He comes across as a spoilsport and is prone to preachiness. As handsome and chiseled as he is, he's too righteous to be much of a romantic. Cap has plenty of allies and legions of admirers, but he cannot maintain an intimate relationship. A visit to the Liberty Bell or a stroll along the National Mall would be his idea of a great first date; his courtship of Bernie Rosenthal in *Captain America* #258 (June 1981) involves a "splendiferously old-fashioned night on the town," dancing to big band music and sharing a carriage ride through Central Park. Cap represents the spirit of America, but not the whole of its soul. He possesses Washingtonian elements (both George and Booker) and his blood pumps to a John Philip Sousa beat, but there's not much Ben Franklin in there, nor Hawthorne or Melville, let alone Presley, Dylan, or Brown—although I bet he appreciates the message of the Godfather of Soul's "America Is My Home."

The best way to get a sense of the sort of man Captain America is and what he stands for is to quote him directly. In a retelling of his origin in issue #255 (March 1981), for example, he reflects, "This land of ours may have seen some hard times, and maybe it hasn't always lived up to the promise of the Founding Fathers . . . but America at its best has always stood for the rights of man, and against the rule of tyrants! And if America needs a man to stand for her principles, to battle the forces of tyranny—then, as God is my witness, I shall be that man!" And from issue #273 (September 1982), this is the sort of thing he tells his foes—in this case, agents of HYDRA: "Like every other tyrant, your lust for power masks your true motive—fear of a free society! For, with freedom, man has pride, dignity, and a sense of destiny. Your fear causes you to arrogantly mock those concepts! You seek to reduce mankind to your own level! But against every despot there has always arisen a champion of liberty! That is why I exist—and why men like me shall always win!"

THE SMARTEST MAN IN THE ROOM

As much as his archnemesis Doctor Doom would dispute it, Mister Fantastic is widely recognized as the smartest man in the Marvel Universe. And that was *before* he gained superpowers. Thanks to cosmic radiation bombarding an insufficiently shielded spacecraft, Reed Richards and his friends gained out-of-this-world abilities. The radiation exposure made Reed's entire body highly ductile, pliable, and resilient. He can elongate any part of his figure remarkable distances and his all-around malleability allows him to alter his shape in unusual ways, so as to mimic a sail or parachute. However, he doesn't engage in sillier sorts of shapeshifting or pose as inanimate objects, as DC's similar-but-goofier Plastic Man will.

Reed Richards sometimes exhibits the philosopher's contempt for bodily concerns. He is the kind of guy who will forget his own birthday (*Fantastic Four* #271, October 1984). He designed for himself the blandest costume in all superherodom: His unitard is functional—and informative, given the "4" on it—and that's all that matters. He does not dye his hair, leaving it visibly gray at his temples. He could use his powers to affect a musculature to rival Captain America's, without any of the training, and he does not bother to. Science doesn't require a six-pack. That Reed Richards won't be defined by his special physical abilities is evident in the alias that he gave himself: While his teammates assumed monikers that describe their superpowers (e.g., "the Human Torch," who can turn to flame), Reed's choice of Mister Fantastic does not highlight his rubberlike qualities. That is because his mind is still more fantastic than his ability to stretch. Even Reed has said that he regards his extendibility as expendable (*Marvel Team-Up* #132, August 1983).

Reed's ability to stretch needs to be understood as not only secondary but also germane to his mental prowess. For instance, his elasticity has been compared to the fluidity of liquid in the context of describing the powers of the Fantastic Four as analogues to the classical four elements (explicitly at least as early as 1981's *Fantastic Four #232*), where he represents water (and the Thing, earth; the Human Torch, fire; the Invisible Woman, air). The view that water is the basic essence of the universe lies at the beginning of both the Greek philosophical and biblical traditions. It was explicitly held by Thales, the first philosopher, and Genesis 1 also seems to suggest that the existence of universal waters predated God's creative activity. And so, his being like water suggests a living, direct, and personal correspondence with the source of all that exists—a correspondence that might, in keeping with science understood in its ancient and contemplative sense, grant him access to thorough knowledge of the whole.

It is also important that the Fantastic Four do not have secret identities. Everyone who matters to Reed is either a member of the Fantastic Four, a superpowered ally, or a hanger-on, so he has no private life to protect. His wife, the Invisible Woman, is more than capable of handling herself; indeed, the conventional wisdom is that her ability to project force fields makes her the most powerful member of the team, physically speaking. All of the discoveries, inventions, and accomplishments of Mister Fantastic are publicly attributable to him—although he withholds some of what he knows and does from the public and even from close friends. Reed has no aspiration to rule, but he is prepared to orchestrate some things from behind the scenes. This degree of discretion and presumption imply that he possesses knowledge of human things as well as inanimate nature such that he can discern what other people should or should not know, for their own good, or for the greater good. No matter how good his intentions, when his secret machinations are exposed, he appears deceitful and conceited. For reasons like these—including the suspicion that he exposed the team to cosmic radiation on purpose—readers have long argued that Reed is a big jerk.

Generally, Reed is lucky to live in a society that values his intellect and leaves him free to conduct his experiments and embark upon his travels, trusting in the goodness of scientific inquiry and exploration, even rewarding him for doing so not only materially but with esteem. Unlike Spider-Man or the X-Men, the Fantastic Four do not typically engender the public's hatred and suspicion, despite having attracted more than their fair share of existential threats to New York City. That said, Reed always takes responsibility for containing whatever trouble follows him home after he goes exploring the Negative Zone, traversing the multiverse, or traipsing through alternate timelines and divergent realities. Overall, he prefers to keep himself isolated from the general public, having few direct interactions with ordinary people on a day-to-day basis—perhaps his least Socratic quality. He's aloof and not terribly warm, somewhat Spock-like in temperament, apt to find monsters and cosmic entities fascinating rather than frightening. He abstracts away from the interests and passions that motivate most people. Even his best friends, Susan and Ben, find his reclusive tendencies and emotional inaccessibility frustrating.

POLITICS, BUT NOT PARTISANSHIP

A useful way to distinguish and compare Captain America and Mister Fantastic is to ask what their homes are. Cap's first home was the military, specifically the army, where a kind of fraternity is established among all members, with a shared sense of duty. His next home is Avengers Mansion, where his teammates become the closest thing he has to family. Their bond is a shared sense of justice and a desire to help and protect innocents. Mister Fantastic's home is with his wife and kids, Franklin and Valeria, plus his best friend and his brother-in-law. They live together in their headquarters, traditionally the Baxter Building, which contains not only their living quarters but also their business offices and reception area, Reed's laboratories, and the team's vehicles and other equipment. They live in close proximity to each other, like true friends should, looking out for each other. The Thing and the Torch may tease and prank each other endlessly, but the entire team shares bonds of love, for each other and for their shared commitment to explore every corner of existence and beyond. Reed does not know how to relax, mentally or physically; I imagine he must have to keep himself taut at all times so he doesn't become a blob. Captain America doesn't relax either. He's always on duty. The armed forces may be set apart from the rest of society, but they're committed to serving the rest of society. The Fantastic Four is also a special unit unto itself, although they do not neglect the interests and cares of the society around them that lets them be who they are and do what they do. They defend society, but as a secondary concern, not as the primary responsibility it is to the army and Avengers alike.

Captain America operated with great latitude as a soldier, going on missions and completing tasks that regular forces could not tackle in regular ways, proceeding on his own initiative to address emerging threats. He exhibits a willingness to do the right thing even when it goes against orders, as depicted in *Captain America: The First Avenger* (2011)—the most unironic and unambiguously patriotic movie about America's fighting forces in recent memory—when he drops behind enemy lines to rescue the Howling Commandos from captivity. He still respects formalities enough to turn himself in afterward for disciplinary action.

The emphasis on Cap's service to America's *ideals* and not just her *interests* becomes even more central to his stories once Rogers is no longer deployed in a theatre of war and he no longer answers to a military chain of command. True, he often maintains official status as an agent of S.H.I.E.L.D., but that's not the same. When former soldiers go into business for themselves, it normally means becoming mercenaries, private security, or other muscle for hire; Cap went in the opposite direction, fighting for intangibles and abstractions such as human rights and human dignity, liberty and equality, answering to nothing but his own conscience. When, in more recent times, the US government has attempted to assert direct authority over him, he has balked and walked. His independence allows him to claim to represent America's ideals, principles, and purposes without being tied directly to the agenda of any specific government and to criticize politicians and policies at home.

What are Captain America's politics? You would expect him to be voted "Most Likely to Be a Conservative" in the superhero yearbook. He comes to us from the past, bringing old-timey morals and manners from a generation before hippies and the pill. He has old-fashioned ideas regarding patriotic duty and sacrifice, decency and formality, hard work and determination, loyalty and integrity, neighborliness and community, personal and interpersonal responsibility, respect for individual liberty, and an earnest optimism about the prospect of liberty for all and the alignment of that outcome with justice. He is "a man out of time," allowing stories to be told that are critical of ourselves today from a perspective originating within our own cultural context; a perspective that is familiar and not foreign, outmoded but not quite obsolete. Having lived through the 1930s and 40s, however, Cap's view of those times isn't romantic or nostalgic; he knows that the past was not unqualifiedly great and can see how we have both declined and progressed since then.

Still, Cap is rarely, if ever, portrayed as a political conservative. Following his revival in the 1960s, he has been a standard New Deal liberal, as Roger Stern put it in the letter column of *Captain America* #246. Stern was writing in 1980, a time when conservatism was on the rise due to the perceived failings of what then passed for big government. The opening sequence of *Captain America: The Winter Soldier* (2014) has Steve Rogers running laps around the Tidal Basin and Reflecting Pool, and every time he passes Sam Wilson, the African-American man who will become the superhero known as Falcon, Cap's sidekick and best friend, Steve says, "On your left." Whether jogging courtesy or subliminal hint, this left-of-center perspective tends to hold that moderate progressivism represents the best interpretation of America's founding and guiding principles and purposes. In practice, this tends to mean subordinating the concern for liberty to an emphasis on equality—or at least working toward equality under the beneficent care of enlightened, competent, and compassionate superiors who promise everybody more freedom one day if only they surrender some more of it for now.

Cap comes from a time when America's foreign interventions were regarded as an unambiguous force for good. He continues to fight for America and Americans even though in many ways they have changed. I don't mean ethnically—

Captain America has always been a friend to all races and an enemy of racism—but ethically, with respect to the character of our souls. He fights on trusting that we are worthy of his efforts and sacrifices, even though it is a fair question whether those who fought in WWII would have been so ready to sacrifice themselves if they could have caught a glimpse of twenty-first-century America. Many of them might have grieved that their sacrifices were wasted—not on account of what we look like outwardly but rather on account of who we have become inwardly. In *Winter Soldier*, Cap seems to wonder whether America knows what it means to be moral anymore, but he continues to fight on its behalf, nevertheless.

Despite being a model of physical, moral, and practical excellence, Cap treats everyone as his equal, possessing high moral worth and dignity, capable of living freely. He leads by example and leaves everyone else free to become as good as they can be, based on the assumption that liberty is universally desirable—a premise challenged by Loki in the first *Avengers* film, claiming that it is natural for human beings to kneel, and Arnim Zola in *The Winter Soldier*, explaining, "Humanity needed to surrender its freedom willingly."

Captain America has expressed wariness about his place as a throwback in today's world, where many Americans believe that nationalism is immoral and our commitments should tilt toward an imagined global community. Other superheroes have moved faster on this front: Superman dropped "the American way" from the list of things he stands for in *Superman Returns* (2006) and renounced his American citizenship in 2011's *Action Comics* #900. The Justice League of America became Justice League International in 1987 before becoming simply the Justice League in 2011, well in advance of the 2017 movie. In the first *Avengers* film, Steve asks, "Aren't the stars and stripes a little old-fashioned?" Putting America first now seems an anachronism; by the end of *Civil War*, Cap has fled America for the hidden African nation of Wakanda. Steve Rogers is not certain that he and America are good fits for each other anymore: In both *Winter Soldier* and in *Civil War*, he is distraught by the degree of concentration of power under government control and the extent to which America has become a surveillance state en route to becoming a police state—something that cannot be blamed solely on presidents of one party or the other.

Presidents, though partisan, are expected to represent all Americans. In representing the idea of America, Captain America should not be overtly partisan, since the raucous but respectful coexistence of countless factions is among the nation's fundamental ideals. His status as an orphan in the care of the state relates to the idea that he belongs to American society as a whole. Half of America may be labeled irredeemably deplorable while another 47 percent is accused of being wholly dependent on a government catering to their every whim, but Captain America is ready shield-in-hand to protect them all and would never dream of denigrating either group like that. Cap should not be right or left or antiright or antileft or even antiright-versus-left. Captain America should defend and rearticulate the American Dream to those on the left and right alike who would declare it dead.

Abroad, Captain America, like his namesake, is at his best when he is a beacon to oppressed peoples everywhere and a symbol of liberty. He might even join them in fighting for their own liberty, providing inspiration and a model to emulate, but he would not come as a conqueror. Captain America does not rule, despite all of his excellences, because he stands for a government based on self-rule, individual and collective. Domestically, Captain America should not run for office because elected officials are stuck in a system divided by adversarial partisanship. He was asked to run as a third-party candidate in 1980's issue #250, but he declined. The alternate Cap of the Ultimate Universe was elected president as a write-in candidate, without campaigning, during a national crisis in 2012, but he resigned the office as soon as national unity had been restored. America may need an extraordinary person to serve as president at a time of national emergency, but it is designed not to need them always and Americans are advised not to crave them. Kingly presidents would destroy everything that America is supposed to stand for. Ideally, Steve Rogers would be chief of a smaller society, like the kings who led the Aegeans on the battlefield at Ilium. But America is nothing like that, meaning that Cap is even more of a man out of time than is usually supposed.

Traditionally, the active life includes participation in the deliberative processes of society, making judgments with respect to which courses of action best serve the common good. But that theory developed when citizens were fewer and involved in politics more personally and directly. In modern mass democracy, most offices go to professional politicians, and most citizens, now numbering in the hundreds of millions, participate in politics less frequently and more indirectly. Even though he stands outside the framework of government—and by representing its ideals, in some sense stands above it—Captain America still represents the idea of public engagement in the pursuit of justice, giving voice to the ideals of free society, serving as inspiration and lending encouragement to individuals to reach their potential, standing up against those forces that impede people's opportunities, and illustrating the need to acquire good practical judgment through practice, experience, and discipline. An optimistic outlook may be helpful but wishful thinking, good intentions, and insistent sentiments are insufficient for finding meaningful success.

Even if Captain America's day job as superhero is abstracted away from day-to-day politics, he is intended to model the qualities of good citizenship in its combination of principles and practices. Cap illustrates the value of loyalty, integrity, seeing the best in others and helping to bring it out, building constructive unity out of diversity, and living in a fashion consistent with and demonstrative of one's dignity. He is fortunate to represent a nation whose principles exceed its laws, allowing people to still be patriotic as they stand up for its ideals of justice while being critical of the current government.

Captain America tries to model the best of humanity within the American context. Because America's exceptional particularity is tied to universal principles, America asserts its specialness while simultaneously denying it. Captain America is intended to represent the best citizen of the best possible regime hewing to the best theoretical principles. He models our dissatisfaction with merely being good neighbors in subpolitical society—the domain of Spider-Man—giving voice to the desire to participate together in the pursuit of the public good as citizens with equal standing, whatever one's background. In his own life he does not pursue much that transcends the political, except to the extent that the politics he represents transcends the particular regime for which he stands. He does not personally concern himself with much that goes beyond our existence as political animals, but he represents allegiance to a view of our political existence that says politics is not the whole of what we are. It is as if he limits himself to the sphere of politics to defend a conception of social life that does not reduce us to our political identities.

TRANSCENDENT TRUTHS

Meanwhile, Mister Fantastic represents the personal commitment to something that transcends our existence as political animals—the pursuit of truth. You can't keep track of all of his PhDs. He was already a supergenius before the accident on the spaceship, but the power to alter the shape of his body, including his brain, has undoubtedly made him exponentially more intelligent. As a modern man, his scientific endeavors proceed along technological directions. Given that his particular mode of truth-seeking involves going on adventures and conducting extraordinary experiments, it is not surprising he runs into a lot of trouble. Those dangers come from the entities he encounters on his escapades, of course, but also from envious, resentful rivals who hope to take him down a peg by pitting their intellects against his, challenging his technology with their own. And so, as befits a comic book character, Reed's life involves a significant amount of action for a man so governed by his brain. Johnny Storm's accusation in the 2005 *Fantastic Four* film—"You always think; you never act"—is unfair; although, if Reed had his choice, he'd rather be thinking. He is not concerned with honor and glory, although he appreciates the respect of other supergeniuses. It is lucky that he also seems to care about innocent bystanders, since his experiments attract a lot of them. Presumably he knows that his ability to do what he does depends on not earning a reputation for irresponsibility on account of excessive collateral damage all across Manhattan.

Given his commitment to seeking knowledge, Mister Fantastic's ability to stretch his body is metaphorically apropos to his principal natural superpower, his intellect. A mind cannot be philosophical or scientific unless it is flexible: plastic enough to absorb new impressions; malleable enough to adapt and expand; able to work its way through or around any obstacle and capable of accessing difficult-to-reach places; but then also capable of reintegrating, recomposing itself, without losing all coherence. A person who seeks wisdom is motivated by wonder, possesses a spirit of openness to novelty and the unexpected, and feels gratitude when corrected; he follows wherever reason and the evidence take him; he does not impose his own preferred conclusions on things prejudicially, whether on the basis of partial opinions regarding the useful, the honorable, the beautiful, or the pious—as if any of those categories could put a limit on what shapes truths may take upon discovery. He must be prepared to look in places that others fear to look, willing to entertain conclusions that were not preapproved, and ready to change in ways that others might find embarrassing or disturbing. A protean quality akin to what Reed's body exhibits is necessary in a philosophical mind.

Reed's aesthetic sense has a classical quality to it; for example, the functional-yet-clunky Fantasticar (aka, the "Flying Bathtub") in which he and his teammates scoot around Manhattan is, from his point of view, beautiful precisely because it suits its purpose perfectly well. The most classical-philosophical person Reed knows would be Karnak of the Inhumans, whose power, to find the flaw in anything such that it may be shattered, is a metaphor for Socrates' mode of argumentation. But as a modern scientist or natural philosopher, Reed's work is tied up with technology in a way that classical philosophy wasn't. He more closely resembles Francis Bacon's model of the scientist than Aristotle's portrait of the philosopher. The classical depiction of the contemplative life included inquiry into what we call the natural sciences, but without the preoccupation with experimentation, engineering, and manufacture that are the defining features of modern science.

The Fantastic Four's headquarters houses a jumble of strange machines and fancy gadgets, though Reed does not publicize all his inventions and discoveries. Some, like the unstable molecules that form the basis of superhero costumes, he shares with the superpowered community, but Reed exercises prudence regarding which knowledge should be shared with nonscientists, for their own sake. He leaves no subject unsubjected to examination—except for magic, which he respects but has only dabbled in, and then only out of necessity (2003's *Fantastic Four* #500). Reed's sticking to the sciences reveals self-knowledge regarding his strengths and weaknesses, even though it means ceding ground to archnemesis Doctor Doom, who combines scholarship and sorcery.

Of course, Reed wonders about whether and how the world might be fixed, and even tries to diagram it out as an intellectual challenge—but he is no reckless revolutionary. Nor is Reed a prophet of some singularity that shall swiftly save us all. His awareness of the complexities of human nature and global systems restrain him from putting any master plan into effect. The stakes are too high to attempt anything as ambitious as social planning without being sure.

In the comics' Ultimate Universe, Reed became a villain and tyrant specifically by deciding to use his genius to rapidly evolve humankind and force society's development into a technological utopia—a project that ultimately failed. At least the main universe's Reed Richards is wiser than that; "Life is a risk," he tells Susan. "We never know from one moment to the next if we will succeed or fail" (*Fantastic Four* #290, May 1986). This is the sort of philosophical modesty missing from those who have too much faith in technology to control and fix everything. It is irrational to expect too much from the application of reason.

How Best to Serve the Community?

Captain America and Mister Fantastic share in common modern commitments that bring the active and contemplative lives closer together, approaching each other in the direction of some middle ground: one a philosophically fashioned man of action; the other a thinker whose activities have significant practical implications.

Cap is not simply a man of action but a man of principle, guided by attitudes that were developed in modern liberal democratic theory, and he is an eloquent spokesperson in their defense. Every virtuous man of action is dedicated to some conception of what is noble that his fellow citizens are supposed to share and uphold, and a related conception of the common good for his community. Cap and America are both committed to universal rights and responsibilities that transcend their political society. America imagines itself as an object of admiration and emulation for the world at large. A commitment to American values also establishes standards by which criticism of America, by Americans, may be advanced without being intrinsically un-American.

Cap believes his interpretation of these principles to be the correct one—as all people tend to do—with such fervor that he has found himself not only clashing with the US government but occasionally giving up his identity as Captain America until America proves it is good enough for him. Even then, however, he doesn't renounce his citizenship or his mission. Instead, he feels the need to stage a one-man resistance against what America has become for the sake of restoring it to what he thinks it should be—as he did in the 1970s as Nomad, and again in the 1980s as The Captain.

Cap reminds us that freedom goes hand in hand with the responsible cultivation of virtuous qualities of character, that a sense of duty toward one's community is different from dependence on, and devotion to, the government, and that we should reject merely materialistic self-interest. He reminds us of the need for free people to exhibit some degree of nobility of spirit to defend their sacred honor and that what unites us is more valuable than what divides us.

America was founded in rebellion against illegitimate authority, but Cap's propensity for distancing himself from America when it fails to live up to his interpretation of its ideals does not make him the best role model for ordinary Americans. He has earned the right to engage in that sort of auto-ostracism because he has proven himself committed to America's defense, has made so many sacrifices on its behalf, and has through long experience acquired good practical judgment to accompany his idealism. The average American, simply, hasn't. His strong dissent deserves due respect on account of the esteem he has earned. Cap's very goodness makes it a mistake to emulate him when he (briefly) turns his back on the country.

When inexperienced idealists who have not demonstrated long commitment to their community appeal to a high-minded sense of justice and presume to stand apart from society—grandstanding in their reproach of America, clamoring for its downfall—they look entitled at best; juvenile, idiotic, and facile at worst. Vehemence, contempt, and pretensions to purity do not sanctify resistance in people who have not exhibited much in the way of prudence, persistence, goodwill, and respect for others.

CHAPTER 4

Captain America may be the best possible citizen in America, in the sense of standing up for America's highest ideals, dedicating his life in word and deed every day for the sake of the well-being of his community. One special thing about America and its ideals, however, is that individuals can pursue happiness in their own way, according to their own conceptions of the best life that are not limited to and may exceed their roles as citizens. Americans are free to busy themselves with matters that traditionally fall short of politics, such as business, and find great success seeking their happiness along that path.

America was founded within the context of a religious heritage that transcends the political too. It was founded furthermore within the context of the enlightenment, where the rational pursuit of truth is of inherent value. Reed Richards is not much of a religious man, but through his scientific pursuit of the truth, he embodies an ideal of the good life that exceeds his role as an American citizen yet does not clash with it. You might say that Captain America lives the kind of life that he lives so that a person like Mister Fantastic can become outstanding in his own way, even with his relative disinterest in politics.

Reed is not the flag-waving sort. He is not preoccupied with being a model American. His allegiance to America is secondary to his allegiance to science. The Fantastic Four's origin story provides incontrovertible evidence that Reed is willing to disregard legitimate authority in his quest for knowledge, given that he had to sneak onto that rocket ship unauthorized, launching it into space without ensuring the safety of the vessel or having gained official clearance. As so many of Reed's supergenius villains demonstrate, brilliant people like to think the rules don't apply to them. Wisdom does not enjoy having to defer to other claims to rule. In an alternate universe where the Nazis won World War II, Reed has to make himself Führer (2012's *Fantastic Four* #605.1), less for ideological reasons than to simply remove any obstacles to seeking knowledge—although, of course, Nazi Reed does try to use his knowledge to fix everything.

Reed respects the order of the cosmos—even when it seems incomprehensibly mysterious and even hostile—more than he values the lives of all living beings. This was evidenced when he saved the life of the world-eater, Galactus (*Fantastic Four* #244, July 1982). The whole truth exceeds merely human priorities and perspectives. Reed's willingness to respect the limits of his own knowledge (#262, January 1984) and allow Galactus's continued existence does not, however, prevent him from stopping Galactus from eating Earth (1966's landmark #50). But Reed's partiality to humankind needs some explaining then, too, doesn't it? Can his solicitude for other members of his biological species be accounted for on purely rational grounds?

PRAISEWORTHINESS, TEMPERED BY ACHIEVABILITY

That Mister Fantastic is familiar with love suggests that reason recommends love, even if it cannot account for the emotion. Reed's morals are conventional and not particularly galvanizing. It is his relationships with his family and friends that keep him grounded. He is at his best when he is sharing his inquiries and discoveries with other remarkable persons whom he admires, such as Tony Stark, T'Challa, and Hank Pym, or when he is cultivating the curiosity of his children or mentoring other brilliant young people in the Future Foundation.

Moreover, his beloved wife, Susan, ensures that he doesn't retreat entirely into the world of the mind. Like Reed, those obsessed with reason ought to be aware of reason's deficiencies—or the conditions of our existence that render rationality alone insufficient for our well-being.

The Fantastic Four is called Marvel's First Family. They accompany Reed on his truth-seeking missions; their personalities and abilities complement his, and his adventures would not succeed without their assistance. His own successes would not be so worthwhile without his family to share them with. He ascends to truth through family, you might say, and from truth back to family. Reed's love for this family rivals his love of truth, and his solicitousness for the rest of humanity is a tertiary concern.

It may seem that Reed's commitment to his family is in tension with his commitment to science, given that science is universal while family is particular. Modern enlightenment morality emphasizes universals, finding partialities potentially unjust. From a cosmopolitan perspective, borders are bad and taking care of one's own is morally suspect. But Reed has more humanistic knowledge than he lets on. His commitment to family exposes the ideological nature of modern trends toward universals. Given the kinds of creatures we are and the kind of world we find ourselves in, it is irrational to forgo partial relationships and seek indiscriminate attachments to all. Relationships of love, which are always personal, must be cultivated in order for us to live well. That is a universal fact about humanity: We are essentially partial beings who can only know so many people and be known well by only some few others in return.

Reasoning about the human condition reveals the need for love, for friendship and companionship—in addition to and beyond our need to cultivate just communities, as Captain America hopes to do. In *Winter Soldier,* Captain America confesses to the Falcon that he is not happy. It is not just that he is too noble for America; he is too noble for his own good. America, the thing that Cap loves, cannot love him back. It is often playing the harlot and letting him down. The thing Mister Fantastic loves most—truth—plays hard to get, but it never disappoints. And his family is always there for him too, even though he can become neglectful of them when lost in his thoughts.

In the lead up to 2015's *Secret Wars* storyline, Captain America objected to the willingness of his fellow heroes (including Mister Fantastic) to sacrifice other earths to save their own. His principles would have led to the destruction of his own planet. The noble person traditionally is willing to die so as not to be dishonored, but Cap is willing to let everyone else die so as not to violate his principles. That is not a model of practical wisdom or classical nobility. After the multiverse collapses, however, it falls to Mister Fantastic, his son and daughter, and the Invisible Woman—a slightly modified twist on the old Trinity—to restore it. Unlike the previously discussed Parallax, who would try to impose his will on creation in the belief he could manufacture the perfect world, Reed is reconciled and resolved to recreating an infinity of imperfect worlds, because that is what freedom and love require, and therefore it is what reason recommends.

We are confronted, then, with the question of which of these two heroes should be regarded as more praiseworthy. Mister Fantastic is more concerned with his studies and his family than he is with everyone else's well-being. His right to mind his own business means he is able to focus on his real passions rather than meddle in everybody else's lives. Captain

America lectures others a lot, telling them what kind of qualities they should acquire so they may enjoy their freedoms more and sustain the social conditions under which everyone has a greater opportunity to do and be what they would prefer. He reminds people that there are some moral commitments that we should share, some efforts that we should make together, and some qualities of character that we should exhibit so that we all may remain free to live as we please.

Today we see, on the one hand, a tendency among many to retreat into unsociable and irresponsible private lives, and on the other hand, a temptation among a growing number to lend credence to illiberal collectivist ideologies and agitate on their behalf in uncivilized ways. As an alternative to those extremes, Cap encourages us to live responsibly, do our part in serving the community voluntarily, and be brave in standing up for each other's freedoms.

Cap furthermore reminds us that we need to heed moral principles and possess a sense of duty so politics does not devolve into a cutthroat pursuit of victory, wealth, and power. Of course, Mister Fantastic reminds us similarly not to seek and admire power for its own sake. The pursuit of power—in his case technological power—needs to be subordinated to the higher standards constituted by reason and love, so it is not used crudely or brutally, even in the name of justice or the relief of suffering.

More people can follow Cap's lead than Reed's, even if nobody can quite live up to his standard. Moreover, from the perspective of preserving liberal democratic society, we need more people to try to follow Cap's lead than Mister Fantastic's. Few people can match Reed's intellectual aptitudes, and he is well aware of that. He wouldn't expect many people to try, or see the utility of trying, and this would not bother him. Cap's sense of self, however, depends on his effectiveness in inspiring people, in reminding and persuading them to live up to the promise and expectations of free society.

In the end, even if it is the case that Reed Richards lives a happier life than Steve Rogers—a life filled with love; a life in which his passion, the truth, cannot let him down like America sometimes disappoints Cap—Mister Fantastic and those like him rely upon the existence of people like Captain America to maintain the social conditions under which they may become as extraordinary as they are. And so, in conclusion, my recommendation would be to be Mister Fantastic if you have the intellectual wherewithal; otherwise, let's agree to prefer Captain America and be grateful for those who dedicate themselves to keeping the traditions of liberty alive. Better than that, try to be such a person yourself—in practice, not only in theory.

And so, in this chapter, the laurels go to the Sentinel of Liberty.

5

Gods in a Longbox

Thor versus Superman

WE BEGAN with the most beastly, earthbound of heroes and are ending in the heavens. Thor and Superman are, arguably, the closest approximations to the divine in the Marvel and DC universes. Thor is a pagan deity given a sci-fi spin, mixed with biblical elements; Superman is broadly biblical in spirit, but with a modern twist. Neither are gods, literally; they are both aliens with godlike qualities. The pagan Thor—a noble hero fighting valiantly on behalf of his community, the Asgardians, defending them against lesser species from lesser realms—is more overtly political. As a paragon of universal morality, Superman rushes to the rescue of anyone on Earth, his adoptive home, and has a reputation as a savior to alien species across the universe. His mission transcends politics; Superman no longer claims to fight on behalf of the American Way and is a citizen of no particular nation. He represents the hope that all humankind may surpass politics and establish peace on Earth. Indeed, the crest on his chest is the Kryptonian symbol for hope.

While Thor used to be partial, centuries ago, to the Vikings who worshipped him, he is now charged with protecting all Midgard (Earth), and he is no stranger to cosmic adventures either. But he is too familiar with the permanence of conflict among people to hope for world peace. He struggles, rather, to remain worthy of fighting on behalf of a worthwhile cause. As a pagan, the worldview in which Thor's stories are set tends to be more tragic. As a character, he is often found flawed and wanting—especially by his imperious father, the Allfather Odin. Superman, like Jesus, has two dads—Jor-El and Pa Kent—and both have every reason to be pleased with him. His world is more comic than tragic. It is ironic, then, that Thor was portrayed as a bit of a boob in 2017's *Thor: Ragnarok*, whereas Superman has been under a cloud of gloom since 2013's *Man of Steel*. Even 2006's *Superman Returns* wasn't all that cheery.

Superman, the first comic book superhero, created for *Action Comics* in 1938 by Jerry Siegel and Joe Shuster, needs no introduction. In addition to comics, he has been featured in newspaper strips, on the radio, on television, in cartoons, and in films since his inception. His bulging biceps, square jaw, and flapping cape set the tone for all superherodom. The most iconic live-action representation of Superman is Christopher Reeve's; his warm rendition and unflappable spit curl in the 1970s and 80s remain unforgettable. The superior pacing and psychology of the dramatic fight scene between Superman and the Kryptonian criminals in 1980's *Superman II*, in comparison with the chaotic climactic battle with General Zod over Metropolis as presented in *Man of Steel*, remains a testament to the obligation to prioritize characterization and storytelling over special effects.

Thor, by contrast, had enjoyed little exposure beyond the comic books—a few animated appearances here and there; an embarrassing live-action outing in the made-for-TV *The Incredible Hulk Returns* (1988)—until Hollywood heartthrob Chris Hemsworth brought him to life in *Thor* (2011), its sequels, and the *Avengers* films. The character first appeared in 1962's *Journey*

Into Mystery #83 in one of the goofiest origin stories that Stan Lee and Jack Kirby ever cooked up, this time with the help of Stan's brother, Larry Lieber. Dr. Donald Blake happens upon Thor's enchanted hammer in a cave, camouflaged as a gnarled piece of Norwegian wood; on whacking it, he becomes the God of Thunder and chases off some stony alien invaders. This patently absurd story was a hit, and soon a modified Norse mythology became familiar to an American audience who, except for aficionados of Wagnerian opera, might otherwise have remained ignorant of it. It was shrewd of Kirby and Lee to choose a Norse god to build a superhero around; he's not too foreign (like an Egyptian or Hindu god would have been) and not too familiar (like a Greek or Roman), meaning they could more freely reinterpret the lore to fit Marvel's purposes.

THE GOD OF THUNDER

Thor stories are equal parts superheroics, fantasy, and science fiction. This founding member of the Avengers does battle with costumed villains like any other superhero. The "Tales of Asgard" sections in early Thor comics fleshed out his fantastical world and backstory. Here, readers were exposed to mythological figures from the extant epics and legends: elves and dwarves, frost giants and fire demons, unusual beasts and mysterious objects of untold power. Stories involved the intrigues among the gods, the constant discord in their foreign affairs, and introduced us to Thor's companions, the Lady Sif and the Warriors Three. Finally, Thor often partakes in escapades in outer space and encounters cosmic beings. These three aspects of his exploits cannot be clearly demarcated, and the best stories—such as the one that introduced Beta Ray Bill, the space-horse who proved worthy of lifting Mjolnir—blend them. It was the mischief of Loki that brought the Avengers together in the first place. Thor regularly confronts supervillains on earth empowered by Asgardian magic. He clashes with the pantheons of other mythologies, or godlike aliens such as the Eternals. The cinematic version of Thor balances all these elements very well: Asgard is both highly futuristic and medieval; the Bifrost Bridge terminates in a space-age transplanetary teleportation contraption not far from where the waters fall off the edge of the world.

In order for Thor to become a superhero, he must don bright garb atypical of Vikings. His winged helm is supposed to add some authenticity, even though Thor needs a helmet like the Hulk needs armor. As a superhero, Thor's moral sentiments are also different from those associated with Vikings, who, in the popular imagination, inflict suffering on others more than they rescue people from it. Odin put Thor in the body of a crippled physician so he would learn humility, a quality prized by other religions but not usually counted among traditional Viking values. A flowery pseudo-Elizabethan dialect furthermore ennobles Thor's manner of speaking; 'tis passing strange, tho' mayhap our valiant Odinson avoideth thereby the reputation for villainy most foul that doth e'ermore attend persons ill-fated to speak with a cursed Nordic tongue.

As in the mythology, Thor wields his famed hammer, Mjolnir, unleashing its full fury on trolls and storm giants and other monsters. Forged of a mystical metal, Mjolnir focuses Thor's powers of weather control, allows him a simulacrum of flight, and imparts to him additional powers like energy blasts and interdimensional travel. Only someone worthy of Mjolnir may hold it aloft, and when it's thrown, it always returns to its wielder's hand. I will note that the ability to control the weather is one of the objectives Francis Bacon identified as among the priorities of modern science—on account of its metaphorical significance as an appropriation of divine powers over invisible, mysterious, and destructive forces. Thor's power set appeals to our desire to be godlike, and to prevent the suffering that God allows and is accused of causing.

As scion of the Realm Eternal and future king of the most resplendent of the Nine Worlds—assuming his adoptive brother Loki doesn't steal the throne first—Thor's circumstances seem to make him altogether unrelatable. But considered metaphorically, Thor offers a model of citizenship relevant to modern society, even if America is no Asgard. We shall discuss Thor's meaning in greater depth later, but consider the fact that hammers are used to build as well as to destroy. We all walk around every day possessing the power to build and destroy, not only physically but with words. Politically, all citizens possess a share of the responsibility for how the state exercises its coercive authority, which may be used to build or destroy, help or harm, and reward or punish. Voting and other privileges of citizenship are therefore kind of like magical hammers.

The Hero of Heroes

I can't imagine that anyone who has read this far into this book needs me to recount the origin of the Last Son of Krypton, or catalog Superman's numerous superpowers. In a very broad sense, every superhero is a riff on the Man of Steel, but that's like saying every hero is a Gilgamesh rip-off or every adventure story is a variation on the monomyth. The courts may have erred when they declared Captain Marvel a copyright infringement, but some superheroes are certainly more like Superman than others. The list of outright analogues to

Superman is lengthy and includes: Apollo, Axiom, Blue Marvel, the Caped Wonder, David Brinkley of Cronk, Diamond, Endymion, Gladiator, Hyperion, Icon, Mighty Mouse, Mister Majestic, Mon-El, Omni-Man, the Plutonian, Samaritan, Sentry, Sun God, Superior, Supreme, Ultraa, Ultraman, Wonder Wart-Hog, and Wundarr the Aquarian.

A common criticism of the Man of Tomorrow is that he is just too powerful, that no threat truly threatens him. How courageous does he really have to be? He's divine according to Aristotle's standards: effortlessly excellent without the need to habituate himself to virtue, therefore exceeding the bounds of ordinary virtue ethics that apply to normal human beings. He has suffered loss, but he isn't blameworthy, such as when Supergirl died in 1985's *Crisis on Infinite Earths* #7, gifting us with one of the most-homaged covers ever. He faces galactic-level threats, such as Brainiac, Mongul, and Imperiex; formidable supervillains on Earth like Metallo and Parasite; and ordinary humans with a penchant for evildoing like Prankster, Toyman, and the crooks of Intergang. One's first instinct might be to say that it is ridiculous to pit Superman against ordinary men armed with dinky little gadgets, but given that not even Darkseid can decisively defeat him, why not? Against the standard that Superman sets, his foes are more equal than unequal. Traditionally, it is said that only Kryptonite can kill Superman—although he is also vulnerable to magic like Mister Mxyzptlk's, as well as red sunlight—but the only time Superman has truly been defeated was when Doomsday just punched him real hard a bunch of times. Even then, Supes was back on his feet a few issues later.

Superman's archnemesis is Lex Luthor, who claims to represent brains, in contrast with Superman's crude brawn. But Superman's powers aren't all muscles and ice breath and laser eyes. Some of his most distinctive abilities pertain to the senses that point in the direction of the intangible—hearing (allowing him to listen in on everyone's supplications or confessions) and vision (telescopic and microscopic, allowing him to see the whole of things and all of its parts). These semidivine powers contrast sharply with Wolverine's heightened corporeal senses of smell and taste. Superman has speech-based powers too—learning many languages, and let's not forget "super-ventriloquism"—all of which speaks to our rational nature. He has an extraordinary memory as well, and he is no dummy, whatever Luthor thinks of him—although, to be fair, his intelligence largely derives from his access to and study of Kryptonian science and technology in the Fortress of Solitude.

And yet, Kryptonian science devolved to dogma, became the basis of extreme social control, and blinded the planet's elders to dangers that would lead to Krypton's sudden demise. Kal-El's awareness of his father's quarrel with the Kryptonian Science Council and the ultimate fate of his birth world probably account in part for why he is an opponent of totalitarian governance on Earth.

Is Superman TOO Good?

Is Superman a good role model for us? It's a trickier question than you might think. On the one hand, as an indefatigable symbol of hope in the eternal struggle between good and evil, we are obliged to recognize him as a great inspiration. As Chris Farley's flabby but surprisingly erudite version of the Hulk put it in the classic "Superman's Funeral" sketch on *Saturday Night Live* (November 21, 1992), "His life was the superhuman expression of the noblest aspirations of man." Superman's appeal does speak to the desire of many people to be like him—or, at least, the desire for there to be people out there who are more like him. His ends are comprehensible and his means are relatable. He fights for this world to bring relief from jeopardy and iniquity. His powers are extensions of our own natural abilities and the abilities we have granted ourselves by artificial means. His morality is familiar enough—imitating him would not require a radical revaluation of our conventional values.

On the other hand, Superman's own phenomenal record of success may count against him as a role model. Ethical behavior isn't just about the struggle to succeed at doing the right thing; it involves properly handling oneself and others in situations where one fails, or when one has been compromised or badly damaged. Those are circumstances Superman rarely confronts. He struggles as he pursues the right thing to do, but the eventual outcome is never much in doubt. As inspiring as Superman can be, his example can be dispiriting, precisely because we find ourselves unable to be as good as him. There are reasons why the ancients argued that men of outstanding virtue have no place within the city. Their tales reflect the difficulties superhumans present: Apollonius Rhodius included Hercules among the Argonauts but then ditched him at the earliest convenience in the story; he so overshadows and overpowers everyone else that if you kept him around, you would realize that you don't even need the other heroes on the mission. That Superman teams with the Justice League is almost a generosity on his part, given that he could take care of most emergencies on his lonesome—as he did handling Steppenwolf in 2017's much-maligned *Justice League* movie.

Superman's surfeit of power and decency means we never see him struggling with whether he should do the right thing, as we all must. It reminds me of the question of how imitable Jesus Christ truly is, given that he was conceived by the Holy

Spirit and lived a life untainted by sin. Superman can turn coal into diamonds, but he refrains from profligacy. He does not seek ostentatious honors. He won't even take a drink.

If anything, his greatest challenge is deciding which competing threats or injustices to confront: Since he cannot be everywhere at once, every decision to rescue someone over here means that a victim over there goes unaided. Every minute spent working on a story for the *Daily Planet* as Clark Kent or sharing a romantic moment with Lois is a minute that someone somewhere on the planet goes without his sorely needed assistance. Lois has even asked him, "How do you even relax and enjoy yourself when you're the ultimate answer to every problem?" (*The New 52: Futures End* #44, May 2015). Superman himself has acknowledged his plight, stating, "On a good, sunny day, I can do anything. So every day . . . whatever happens . . . it's kind of *always* my fault" (*Batman/Superman* #9, June 2014).

This dilemma is something his stories must lampshade; dwelling upon it would undermine the conceit of his double life and the way his alter ego allows him to seem more accessible to us. It's the comic book version of the theodicy conundrum; dwelling on it results in precisely the sort of attitude that blames God for the evil that human beings do. Maybe Clark just knows you can't take care of others unless you take good care of yourself.

Still, he could put his army of Superman robots on constant patrol worldwide to prevent every injury and right every wrong, could he not? Refraining from doing so makes him more like the biblical God and Jesus than less, in that they don't abolish all suffering either even though in theory they could. Suffering in this world must not be the worst possible thing, then, though that conclusion may seem callous. Superman leaves people generally free to be responsible for themselves—modeling good behavior for them, rather than alleviating them of the need to practice it.

Superman's goodness is related to his great fortune—something that compromises his ability to seem like a plausible role model for those who are less fortunate. As regards both nature and nurture, he has little reason to complain. Sure, his home planet blew up; but he was the lone survivor (until Supergirl, the Kandorians, and some others showed up), so that's pretty lucky. He was discovered and dearly loved by Ma and Pa Kent—a more Rockwellian parentage you will not find. He grew up in idyllic Smallville rather than a crime-ravaged city or evil empire. Superman is well liked by good people, has an amazing wife and successful career, and cannot plausibly claim any victimhood status—despite having to keep his true self closeted. Even if it weren't for his superpowers, his character has been formed by such a favorable environment—full of love, under a just legal regime, littered with opportunity and positive experiences—that his life's circumstances cultivate in him an inclination toward virtuous action that he cannot take full credit for.

In these ways, Superman is decidedly different from Thor, who had to prove himself worthy of wielding Mjolnir, has a treacherous brother always causing him grief and goading him into trouble, and is constantly castigated by an imperious father whose favor he is ever at risk of losing and needing to regain. Odin often is so dreadfully disappointed, whereas Jor-El and Lara and Ma and Pa Kent have only ever had reason to be proud. Lara feigned disappointment that her beloved son would want to experience mere humanity for himself in *Superman II*, but she must have anticipated how he would learn from the experience and be better for it. She lied when she told him that the crystal chamber would strip him of his powers irreversibly, presumably to see what he was willing to give up for love, trusting that he would eventually recognize his mistake and reclaim his heritage to best serve all of humanity. She knew his love for all people would prevail in the end over his love for just one person—giving Lara reason to be prouder still.

GREAT POWER VERSUS PERSONAL RESPONSIBILITY

Faith in the modern doctrine of progress, articulated in the philosophy of Immanuel Kant, is embedded deeply and vibrantly displayed in yarns about the Big Blue Boy Scout. This doctrine maintains that it is reasonable to believe that if we resolved to behave morally, not expediently, we could dispense with the need for divine providence, eliminate suffering, and live together in harmony worldwide. In comic books, it is certainly possible to tell stories that lend credence to this view. Even when Superman falls short of these ideals—as in 1988's *Superman* #22, where he killed versions of General Zod and the criminal Kryptonians—it only served to afterward reaffirm his optimism: He vowed never to kill again, suggesting that he should have been able to find another way (*Adventures of Superman* #450, January 1989).

Superman's vow implies that he believes there are no no-win scenarios. Superman intends to show humankind the truth of this principle through his actions. It's a lesson echoed by his father. "Let your actions and ideals become a touchstone against which mankind may learn how to serve the common good," Jor-El says in *Superman: The Movie* (1978). "They can be a great people, Kal-El. They wish to be. They only lack the light to show the way. For this reason above all—their capacity for good—I have sent them you." Apparently, the Light previously sent by another Father doesn't count, or needs replacing. He wasn't sufficiently concerned about humankind's potential on Earth, to be achieved through righteous works. Jor-El advances a similar position in *Man of Steel:* "You will give the people of Earth an ideal to strive towards. They will race behind you; they will stumble; they will fall. But in time, they will join you in the sun, Kal. In time, you will help them accomplish wonders." Superman, then, shows us that we could save ourselves if only we were so resolved, with enough hope and the best intentions.

That Superman is a messiah figure grounded in the biblical tradition is not a novel insight. In *Superman: The Movie,* Kal-El starts his tutelage under Jor-El at the age of eighteen and it lasts twelve years, making him thirty years old when he begins his mission on Earth as Superman—the same age as Jesus when he starts his ministry (Luke 3:23). In that film, Jor-El tells him, "You shall carry me inside you all your days," adding, "The son becomes the father; the father becomes the son"— and then, really on the nose, says: "I have sent them you, my only son." In *Man of Steel,* Clark is thirty-three years old when he prepares to sacrifice himself to save the world—the same age as Christ upon his crucifixion—a decision made with a stained-glass Jesus casting light on him. When Superman dies in *Batman v Superman: Dawn of Justice*, he is flanked by crosses formed by the rubble around him.

These are but a sampling of the ways in which scripture is pillaged for the purposes of the Superman mythos. It is a larger question, however, whether Superman is simply derivative of Jesus, a distortion of him, or a criticism of and replacement for him. Related to that question: Is the doctrine of progress just the secular side of the Christian message, or its subversion through an appropriation of its language and values? The answer to that question is complicated by the very fact that much of Christianity nowadays has embraced the good news of the modern doctrine of progress despite the vanity of searching the New Testament for evidence to vouch for it, and despite the questionable religious credentials of its original intellectual proponents and loudest ideological advocates.

Peace on earth is something to pray for, but there is no assurance in scripture that the attempt to live righteously by following Jesus will result in the establishment of peace and justice in this world. Success in this world is, however, the express promise of following Superman's example. One downside of too strict a faith in enlightenment romanticism is that if all our best efforts to save the world do not pan out, we have only ourselves to blame. We must not have been good enough or tried hard enough. Our disappointment and frustration breeds impatience, cynicism, and accusation. The emphasis on forgiveness in Christianity is tied to a recognition of our permanent imperfections; but given an expectation of eventual perfection, continued failure is not so forgivable.

Christians are supposed to be pilgrims in this world, not really belonging to it, whereas Superman is an immigrant to this world, and he wants to belong to all of it. In 1983's *Justice League of America* #212, Superman, battling some alien invaders, declares, "They're going to learn what it means to harm the world I've adopted! For when they harm that world, when they harm one man or one woman of the human race—they've harmed the people and things I love—and I just—won't—stand for it!" Note here that while, technically, the Kents adopted him, Superman speaks as if he were the one who adopted all of humanity. In *Superman II*, Zod remarks, "I've discovered his weakness. He actually cares for these Earth people"—to which Ursa responds, quizzically, "Like pets?" In 2003's *Superman: Birthright*, Superman is a vegetarian because the death of any animal disturbs him as much as the death of a human being. When he stands so far above humanity that the moral distance between us and any other species becomes negligible, it is understandable that Superman regards himself as transcending the ordinary politics of this world.

The big question is, why isn't Superman king of the world? Clearly, it would be wrong for him to be *tyrant* of the world— that's why the recent *Injustice* video game and comic book franchise is called precisely that. It is why he entrusts Batman with Kryptonite, so he can be taken down if he ever goes rogue (*Action Comics* #654, June 1990; also *Wonder Woman* #219, September 2005). But given how good and capable he is, why not be king—the sort of ideal benevolent monarch wished for by those who believe democracy has failed?

The idea that Superman may be worthy of being king has been hinted at. In *Man of Steel*, when Clark imagines an idealized version of himself in a virtual-space conversation with Zod—who, nota bene, sports a Caesar haircut—he is wearing a Kansas City Royals jersey. In the comics, the Metropolis major league baseball team is called the Monarchs. And what's more American than baseball?

The reason why Superman does not make himself king must be that he respects people's freedom too much. He may not want to say anymore that he stands for the American Way, but insofar as he recognizes that free people should not have a king, he does so implicitly. American republicanism was in part founded on a recognition that the only king people should have is their Lord in Heaven and of the World to Come; it is and shall be good and just to serve and worship that King; but in the interim, here on earth, no man or woman deserves that much devotion or dominion.

In *Superman IV: The Quest for Peace* (1987), Superman attempted to exert authority over all the sovereign nations of the world, showing up at the United Nations and declaring that he was unilaterally dismantling the world's nuclear arsenals. The most unrealistic thing about this intervention was that the UN ambassadors there cheered and celebrated. By film's end, however, Superman learned that he cannot establish peace on Earth by force. The people of the world must learn to want it enough to implement it themselves.

In 1994's *The Spectre* #22, Superman observes, "I took responsibility for my own acts. Humanity should do the same. There is a danger in beings such as ourselves assuming too much responsibility." Free people govern themselves. The problem is that freedom is hard, and there will always be people who yearn for kingly individuals to rule over them. At the core of the American regime is the noble lie that all human beings want to be free; however, in reality, not everybody prefers liberty to submission. In light of how difficult liberty with responsibility is, many people would prefer dependence to independence, especially if the former could be made easy and pleasant. We are so given to irresponsibility that we'll insist our inherently risky behavior should be somehow without peril—think of how Lois Lane keeps putting herself in precarious situations because she trusts Superman will rush to her rescue every time. The problem with Superman, therefore, isn't that he might want to make himself king; it is that too many people would *want him to be* king and wouldn't mind being kept "like pets." Therefore, a desire for Supermen or Superwomen is a declaration that the American experiment in self-government has failed.

THOR, GOD OF THE MIDDLE CLASS

At least Superman doesn't pretend to be an actual god, like Thor does. For those in the Judeo-Christian tradition, admiring such an individual presents a problem: The Bible condemns, in no uncertain terms, those who aspire to godhood and those who admire false gods. It's *literally* the First Commandment. Even among the relatively godless, the judgment that some-body is trying to "play God" is supposed to be damning. Thor, thankfully, makes no pretensions to perfection. "I make grave mistakes all the time," he admits in *Ragnarok*. As a pagan deity, Thor has appetites and impulses that resemble our own. Unlike Jesus, Thor is susceptible to temptation and otherwise blun-dering. Jesus calms storms; Thor starts them. The guardian of Midgard, Thor has vast powers over the forces of nature on Earth partly on account of his mother being the earth goddess Gaea (*Thor* #301, November 1980). In Norse mythology, Thor's mother is Jord, a Norse giant, or *jotun*, who is said to personify the Earth. Thor retains a desire for glory won in battle and is always prepared to confront and destroy any of Earth's, or Asgard's, enemies—rather than, say, love them.

Thor's father in Asgard requires the Thunder God to prove himself constantly. This teaches him that his "worthiness is not an absolute condition," but rather, "something for which even a god must never stop striving" (*Unworthy Thor* #4, April 2017). An angry Odin will relent in time, but not without being appeased. All told, Thor's character and relations are relatable to us mortals. As a superhero, Thor wants to help people, but he doesn't want to be worshipped by them (*Thor* #330, April 1983). Thus, we may consider him a possible role model, whatever theological baggage he brings. For this chapter it is more important to discern his ethical and political significance than to quibble over religion.

That Thor is a prince gives his stories an immediate political significance. Just as his purported godhood makes him potentially problematic, we may wonder whether his status as a prince makes him unsuitable for admiration and emulation in our supposedly meritocratic liberal democracy. But admiring aristocratic qualities of character does not equate to longing for the reestablishment of aristocratic social and political orders. Alexis de Tocqueville argued that democracies could learn a lot from aristocracies and aristocrats, and comic books have long recommended noble kings, princes, and princesses as possible role models, from Black Panther to Aquaman and Wonder Woman.

Thor's stories address what it means to be worthy of ruling, or participating in rule; how to govern others as well as oneself. Thanks to an enchantment on Thor's hammer, it can only be lifted by those deemed "worthy," implying that people should be admirable if they are to possess power. Every citizen of a democratic republic should recognize that they possess some share of the power and privileges that historically belonged to royalty and aristocracy. They share the same responsibility to use their power well on behalf of their community. They ought to be worthy of that power. We will even strip some of the privileges of citizenship from convicted felons who prove themselves unworthy.

We don't routinely assess every citizen's worthiness of the powers and privileges that citizenship bestows, however, preferring to default, democratically, to a recognition of their entitlement to them. Still, we know that the republic won't long survive the corruption of its citizenry. Thor may therefore be seen as a metaphorical role model for republican citizenship, where every citizen is understood as a sort of little prince, enjoying rights, liberties, and responsibilities that only elites possess in more restricted regimes.

Modern liberal democracy, with its commercial markets and technological capabilities, does not ask for a great deal of nobility from its citizenry. It mainly allows people the opportunity to rise to a higher station if they find ways to help other people get more of what they want and enjoy. But we object to people succeeding dishonorably, and nobody is supposed to merit success on their own assertion. People are expected to prove themselves worthy of their success, to earn it.

When people obtain their success in a fashion that seems undeserved and at the expense of everybody else—whether in Washington or on Wall Street—the entire system falls into disrepute. Those who fall behind will themselves seek undeserved success in undignified ways or else protest the whole arrangement. When this happens, the citizenry's ability to identify and locate a suitable leader to clean up the mess will have been significantly compromised. Thus, citizens have a responsibility to cultivate some nobility of character and an interest in seeing it exhibited in those around them, especially in those above them.

The Declaration of Independence makes explicit reference to the "sacred honor" that its signatories pledge—something presumed to be owed to all free and rational persons to whom that document is addressed, and something that all citizens are encouraged to uphold. The concern for nobility and honor that motivates Thor is not foreign to a democratic society, however outdated and outmoded that language may sound to democratic ears. A cynical person might sneer at the language of honor and the expectation of noble behavior in citizens and their representatives, as if that were mere rhetoric—but only to everyone's detriment in the long run. To discourage or dismiss considerations of honor in public affairs is to embrace despotic and slavish behavior and admit that power is its own justification and the only reality—a situation that renders all talk of justice meaningless, all consideration of the common good a sham.

Thor may be a prince by birth, but he does not crave the power to rule; he wants to help and to serve. At the end of *Thor: The Dark World* (2013), he says he "would rather be a good man than a great king." The challenge facing Thor, to be worthy of Mjolnir, or to be worthy of being king someday, is not altogether different from the challenge facing young people who will grow up to enjoy the rights and privileges of citizenship. They are entitled to them whether they prove worthy of them or not; but boy, wouldn't it be preferable if they were worthy of them? In *Thor: God of Thunder* #17 (March 2014), Thor is referred to as "a god who wondered every day if he was worthy, without realizing that was the very thing that made him so." Woe to America if its young citizens ever came to see themselves as simply entitled to their rights and privileges, rather than feeling impelled to demonstrate their worthiness of them.

It is worth noting that, historically, among the Norsemen who worshipped the gods of Asgard, Thor was most popular among the middle class of freemen—fishermen, farmers, merchants, blacksmiths and other craftsmen, and soldiers—comprising the majority of the populace. (Nobles, naturally, worshipped Odin.) He was their defender and protector. He did not have a reputation for being particularly smart, and he was quick to anger and resorted to brute force, but he did not stay angry long. Thor seems to be a suitable hero for a nation that is intended to be governed by its middling element, a nation whose collective well-being is cast in terms of how well its middle class thrives, at the mercy of neither the too rich or the very poor. That Thor is a role model for average people and not just the elites is further confirmed in the comics by the demon Mephisto, who rages at the nobility Thor inspires in ordinary men, reducing the ranks of souls that descend to his realm (*Thor* #310, August 1981).

Within a free society there are going to be people who do not live so honorably or nobly, people who believe that their rights come without responsibilities, people who treat their fellow citizens like enemies to be defeated or exploited. Citizens who are more scrupulous do not have the right to simply expel these cads from the community; it falls instead to them to endeavor to persuade these others to live and contribute to society like citizens ought to.

Thor's opposite is his brother, the trickster god Loki. Admittedly, Loki has been portrayed sympathetically in both comic books and films, where handsome Tom Hiddleston makes him out to be a lovable rogue. From Loki's own point of view, he can claim to be the victim of discrimination and prejudice: He is never treated like an equal among the other gods, and there is a glass ceiling that prevents him from ever becoming king. Loki is the victim of Asgardian aggression and ethnic assimilation; a frost giant by birth, he's forced to hide his true form through techniques of body modification. Even then he will never truly fit in, condemned to being the Other in perpetuity. However, Thor still loves Loki and hopes that someday he will forgo his evil ways and live nobly, like the prince he is, and be more than the God of Mischief.

Loki is like the citizen who looks out only for himself, for personal gain, without concern for his reputation. He would seize the throne and rule despotically if he could; in this, he resembles those who would install their agents in seats of power to extract whatever they can from everybody else for their own advantage, using whatever words (or magic spells), whatever ruses (or charms), and whatever arms will bring others under their thrall. This is the sort of person who ridicules every pretense to nobility, the type that champions the nihilistic will to power over common decency and kinship. Loki represents the desire to rule not by lifting oneself up to a higher level but rather by bringing everybody around and everything great down and forcing them to bow to him—the spirit of envy and resentment and bitterness and vengeance.

In the first *Avengers* movie, Loki says that human beings belong on their knees. It is the responsibility of human beings to prove him wrong by refusing to bend the knee and by not forcing others to bend a knee. But as misery loves company, so too do the Lokis of the world ally themselves with similarly devious and disgruntled types, convincing them that the smart thing to do is to join against those pompous buffoons foolish enough to still maintain a sense of personal integrity, those dolts who retain some hope that their community might be worthy of their devotion and sacrifices. Of course, for Thor to be Thor, he needs a Loki to overcome, proving himself thereby worthy of his station. In a sense, then, it is lucky that honorable citizens will never be short of dishonorable types to vie against in the struggle to keep their community free. The proliferation of Lokis is the price of freedom.

Where is Odin in this analysis? Isn't there a problem with reading Thor metaphorically as a citizen in free society, so long as he still has a king to heed? The answer is that Odin is like the Founding Fathers. He did not simply inherit the throne; he had to fight for it and make sacrifices to earn it. His hands are not perfectly clean, and many of his qualities and actions look morally dubious in hindsight, though they were necessary to bring about a golden age in Asgard. Odin needs to arrange things so Thor can become the kind of person capable of ruling Asgard well.

Similarly, Americans were given institutions intended to require people to gain the experiences that build the sort of character that is worthy of freedom and capable of guarding and enlarging it. The Founders still tower over America like Odin does Asgard; like Odin's decrees, the feeling of their continued influence chafes. The orders they established to ward off tyranny seem obsolete and inconvenient when they frustrate our desires to get what we want, because we're sure we know better now.

Like the Founders, Odin wants successors who will uphold the integrity of the regime he built, which requires a mixture of pride and humility. To that end, Odin puts Thor to the test, constantly, to ensure that he is worthy of the powers and privileges to which he was born. If, instead, you wanted to make a free people unfree by degrees, you would gradually save them from such arduous efforts, exempting them from the expectation that they attend to the public business, or reducing their opportunities to do so, such that they feel no need to acquire the virtues of citizenship. Instead, allow them to become convinced that there is no limit to what they are entitled to and nothing they are expected to do to merit it. They would give themselves over to the little Lokis within their souls so that the bigger Lokis out there could subdue them with ease. Looking to Thor as a role model means refusing to let that happen; it means being able to say, "I say thee nay!" and then strive "For Asgard! For Midgard!"

Lo, There Shall Come a Reckoning

As with chapter four, the contest in this chapter is a dispute between what is best in theory and what is better in practice. I confess that one thing I don't like about my criticism of Superman is that it acknowledges Lex Luthor has a point: The existence of someone like a Superman—or simply even the yearning among people for there to be a Superman—belittles humanity. If Superman is to be admired and imitated because he is like Jesus, then it would be better to simply admire and imitate Jesus. If he is to be admired because he is better than Jesus, then we admit that we would be right to defer to outstanding individuals in all things in the hope they will cure the world of injustice and suffering. Either that, or we should resolve to form of ourselves a collective army of Supermen. But that sounds too much like what the totalitarian governments that arose in the twentieth century claimed they were trying to do.

However, I cannot simply award the victory to Thor over Superman. Superman really is the most super of superheroes, and more divine than Thor. But I think Clark could be convinced that for the sake of humanity he should withdraw from the competition—perhaps by his friend Diana, avatar of love and peace, more divine still than he—since putting his own example on too high a pedestal risks dehumanizing the people he claims to love. He has nothing to gain or prove by winning, after all. In a competition with Thor, I like to imagine that Superman would step aside and let Thor win by forfeit. Which would humble Thor. Which is exactly what he needs.

Let Thor then be the victor in this contest.

CONCLUSION
Contestation of Champions

THE HEROIC IMPULSE

FOR A LOT of people today, superhero stories are where they first encounter questions that ask what kind of life they should lead, what kind of character they should exhibit, and how they can contribute to their communities. So it is not out of place for us to investigate superhero stories to find out what they recommend. An analysis of popular culture can tell us a lot about who we think we are or should be. Plato had no compunction about considering examples from Homer amid his arguments. While the exploits of Achilles, Diomedes, and Odysseus are less well known today, the Avengers and Justice Leaguers serve as capable stand-ins. The desire to save the world and admiration for those who endeavor to do so have not disappeared. The heroic impulse has not withered away in our age even though physical expressions of courage are often discouraged and shows of moral superiority seem unseemly.

Having examined ten leading superheroes, we are now in a position to assess what they can teach us about how to save our world, our society, and ourselves. Our friendly-but-critical perspective on these heroes allows us to diagnose our own flaws and deficiencies, and by reading them generously and metaphorically, we can consider whether their popularity is a sign of something healthy or unhealthy in us.

WHAT DO YOU WANT TO FIX?

If you think the biggest problem today, ethically speaking, is the abrogation of personal accountability, even the outright inculcation of irresponsibility in people, then Wolverine's personal ethic is something to admire. Wolverine's focus is less on finding fault and spreading blame and more on taking responsibility for cultivating a stronger character—one that can assist others in overcoming the difficulties they face in their own lives too. Taking responsibility for the kind of person one becomes is a vital prerequisite for voluntary action, living with dignity, and treating other people with respect by recognizing the same capacity within them. It is the basis of meaningful self-esteem, essential for achieving happiness worthy of pride or maintaining pride despite being deprived of the conditions for happiness.

Wolverine's example is appealing if you think society has gone awry by infantilizing people, promising freedom from pain and hardship, liberating them from consequences or expectations, and excusing them on account of misfortune. Admittedly, admiring Wolverine for these reasons seems insensitive; nobody likes the jerk who unsympathetically says, "Chin up, pun'kin." But Wolverine's attitude is hardly indifferent to the suffering of others; he is principally motivated to assist others who suffer. He furthermore serves as a cautionary tale for people infected by a righteous bloodlust, overly excited by the prospect of destroying those whom they find odious.

If you think the biggest problem today is that civil society has evaporated—that the state has squeezed out social institutions and people find or take too few opportunities to practice cooperation and perform kindnesses in their social relations—then Spider-Man is the hero you're looking for. Spider-Man represents an appeal to restore social capital, rebuild relationships of trust, and come to each other's aid, rather than retreating from your community into private life and preferring to rely on public assistance instead of private generosities in times of need. He's a bowling together hero in a bowling alone world: If you have ever lived in a city of millions without feeling an ounce of neighborliness, or felt like people hew to some tacit agreement to proceed throughout the day as if other people don't really exist, then Spider-Man recommends friendliness and a helping hand, even toward strangers, as a starting point. Unfortunately, being a good neighbor is not richly rewarded by society, and surrounded by selfishness and corruption, the person who makes a sincere effort to be neighborly can look ridiculous or get squashed like a bug for making everybody else look bad.

If what Wolverine and Spider-Man represent, mainly, are appeals to reconstitute ourselves ethically on subpolitical levels, then Captain America and Thor focus our attention more on our roles as members of political society. That their counsel to us is complementary is reflected in the way these two characters are so friendly with each other. It is a comic book cliché that superheroes always stumble into fights with each other, but Cap and Thor have hardly ever squared off in over fifty years of storytelling. Thor's hammer and Cap's shield meet in a loud clang when they first interact in the films. Cap successfully coordinates an exhilarating team effort to subdue Thor in *Ultimates 2* #5 (June 2005). But these two heroes have rarely clashed, and that fact is noteworthy.

Captain America stands up for everyone's rights, and especially our liberties—the freedom to live as we please, enjoy what we like, say what we think, be who we are, do what we do, and contribute to society as we see fit. America is the regime that endeavors to embody these rights and freedoms, but they belong to all human beings in accordance with our universal nature: America and her captain are merely beacons. These rights recommend democratic forms of government because nobody is the boss of anyone else by nature. Any nation that respects these rights needs to protect itself against those who would suppress or deny them. There are individuals and nations for whom the failure of regimes premised on human rights would be a cause for celebration, whether for reasons of ideology, glory, wealth, or power. It is not enough for America to command forces to defend itself from tyrants and other external threats. It needs to maintain a citizenry that is actively involved in replicating itself as a body capable of continued self-governance.

If you think the biggest problem society faces today is the degree of divisiveness exhibited by its citizens, then Captain America is a good role model to adopt. He represents what unifies all Americans over what divides them. He appeals to the abstract principles that all Americans are supposed to endorse even when they disagree about specific policies. This emphasis on unity makes the most sense when America is at war. The last time a strong feeling of unity brought Americans together followed immediately after the attacks of 9/11, but one should not want to rely on conditions like those. Moreover, given how polarized America has become even though 9/11 still casts its shadow, it appears that one cannot depend on unity enduring even when galvanized in that fashion.

And some division, respectfully undertaken, suggests a healthy polity. Captain America's story is intimately entangled with the struggle against totalitarian regimes that prioritize the collective over the individual, seeking to manufacture a robust national unity. Attempting to rigorously enforce a substantial sense of national unity is not compatible with freedom. Free people exhibit differences that take the shape of disagreements, even prejudices. In the presence of such diversity, even where there is goodwill, a deep and thick form of unity can only be realized through imposition, exclusion, and excision. It is irrational to expect even decent and reasonable people to join in lockstep. As a result, postpartisanship proves difficult to distinguish from hyperpartisanship, in which it is insisted that partial views and favored values be embraced by all as whole truths and complete virtue.

Under these conditions, a demand for unity becomes imperious, disrespectful, and guaranteed to antagonize. When each person's opportunities to interact, cooperate, and compromise with others have been compromised, people retreat into ideological bubbles and become convinced that their own views are wise and good, ready to go on the offensive against anybody who disagrees. Dissenters are expected to recant and conform, their recalcitrance serving as evidence of their ignorance and intransigence. At a time when everything is highly politicized, symbols of unity, such as Captain America, sadly run the risk of exacerbating conflicts instead of ameliorating them.

Is it possible for citizens to behave with dignity and exhibit respect for each other in spite of their differences, despite their arguments and rivalries? Given the crass name-calling and mean-spirited misrepresentation that now characterizes our public discourse, this may seem like too much to ask. We would have to expect less from politics, realizing that not all problems have political solutions, and so stop waging total political war in the belief that crushing our enemies will bring about justice and happiness. It would mean regarding the process as more important than the outcomes—important for how we shape ourselves and our relationships.

The uncivil way we behave toward each other is made worse by politics being reduced to a corrupt power play where, whichever side wins, a dishonorable elite will secure obscene gains for themselves while leaving the peons to fight over table scraps. If you believe this to be society's most pressing problem, then I would recommend Thor as a suitable role model. I recognize that there is a side to Thor that comes across as a bumbling oaf who sees every problem as something to be struck with the bluntness of a hammer, but I would emphasize the side of Thor that recommends to all people that they should aspire to live more nobly, treating themselves and each other in a more dignified fashion.

It is true that Thor will battle demons and trolls and giants—existential threats to Asgard on account of their constant assaults upon the Realm Eternal. And while Asgard has its occasional malcontent beyond the scheming Loki, such as the alluring Enchantress, it enjoys mostly concord among its citizens—whom the movies wisely depict using actors of all races. As regards humanity, with all *its* diversity, Thor treats every human being as worthy of respect, as a creature with dignity, deserving his aid and inspiration. He speaks to them in the same manner that he addresses his fellow Asgardians. Villains who would prey upon human beings will find themselves challenged by Thor, but the proportion of humanity that he sees as in need of a hammer blow or lightning bolt is very small, and they represent no particular identity or collective interest.

Thor is a prince who models princely behavior for ordinary human beings, so they may learn to reflect princely behavior themselves despite their lack of noble rank. Thor tends to treat the United States as his home base on Earth, a regime dedicated to the fundamental premise of equality, yet one that grants enough freedom so every person may seek to become the best possible version of him- or herself. Freedom implies the opportunity to excel; but however excellent one becomes, we are still expected to treat each other with the respect due to equals. That said, an insistence on equality alone keeps individuals stunted and incapable of being much use to others. Inequalities are not inherently objectionable, but people should be discouraged from acting like the excellences they develop give them the right to treat their fellows like inferiors.

Thus, the possibility of maintaining such a regime is intrinsically tied up with treating each other with a high level of respect, even though not everyone deserves the same degree of admiration. This is not terribly different from the way aristocrats are supposed to treat each other. Democratic people are rightly averse to oligarchical behavior, but some aristocratic behavior helps preserve democracy—or, at least, the kind of democracy worthy of our commitment. When each side believes their cause to be altogether noble and their opponents to be altogether base, compromise between the parties becomes impossible and coexistence becomes strained. In a democratic society, one debases oneself when one debases another; when we reduce other people to caricatures of themselves, we only make caricatures of ourselves. People should at least maintain the appearance of treating each other as worthy of respect, in a spirit of generosity. No amount of sneering and jeering on social media ever made anyone, whether on the giving or the receiving end, a better person.

I recommend Thor as a model of dignified comportment because his (nonsuperpowered) behavior is largely within our reach. It does not depend on some far-reaching, fundamental, system-wide change before anyone can attempt it. Aiming to present a more dignified version of oneself, and treating others properly, is something anyone can try. To emulate the nobility of Thor within a democratic context is to invite other free people to do so as well. Not everyone will be converted, but hopefully enough will be that the regime does not devolve into a vulgar contest for power and lucre used to reward one's friends and harm one's enemies.

What I am describing doesn't require ornate and ostentatious raiment. It also does not require Shakespearean flair— although the ability to articulate oneself intelligently in public is something that every citizen in a free society should cultivate in themselves, in part because that is what is necessary to show respect to others. To start, it is enough to avoid coarseness and calumny in one's daily interactions.

Please don't mistake my recommendation to treat others with whom one disagrees with greater respect for foolish naiveté, wimpiness, or wishy-washiness. Nobility of spirit comes from a position of confidence and resilience; it expects respect to be shown in return. It retains a readiness to fight when a battle needs engaging, but it doesn't provoke unnecessarily. It doesn't take offense too easily, and it doesn't mistake all disagreement for attack either. Furthermore, a noble spirit isn't humorless or joyless: Thor appreciates a good jest, even recollecting with good humor some pranks Loki has played on him; he likes friendly competition, like an arm-wrestling match with Hercules; and he'll enjoy a barrel of mead from time to time with friends or strangers.

A VICTOR, CROWNED

It would be preferable to say that all four of the heroes who made the final cut should form a team to serve as role models for us in the personal, social, and political dimensions of our lives. (And, indeed, all four have served as members of the Avengers at one time or another.) I would furthermore recommend aspects of the other superheroes discussed in this book, plus traits belonging to many other superheroes who would not have been overlooked if I had another hundred pages. But the cover of this book promises that a victor shall be declared. And so, under the present circumstances, Thor wins this contest as the exemplar of what we most need now—a noble model for citizens such that they may preserve their freedoms in an honorable fashion, and not regard that prospect as irretrievably lost.

If a dignified public space has become unsalvageable, however, then Spider-Man's neighborliness and Wolverine's integrity would be what remain to us, allowing us to take what responsibility we can for ourselves and those nearest to us. But as with Spider-Man, that life is one that is reconciled to being down on your luck; and as with Wolverine, it not only threatens to become solitary and brutish, but in the absence of a community with shared standards of the honorable, one's own discipline and dedication to others seems subjective and arbitrary. Surely, that is a much too bleak assessment of our lot, even if there are reasons to be pessimistic about our prospects for the ennoblement of our souls. Certainly, Thor is not one to retreat, forfeit, or lose faith. If you were to express the intention to give up on everyone, he would surely have words with thee.

I keep my recommendations modest (and hopefully not too sanctimonious) because pretending to have divined how to save the world would exceed even my capacity for suspending disbelief. Any proposal to save the world involves treating an irreducibly complex situation as if it were a problem amenable to simple solutions, achievable with sufficient imagination, commitment, and means. We might imagine that an all-knowing, all-good god might be capable of saving the world, but we flawed and partial human beings are fooling ourselves when we believe we can do it.

These days, some people hope that the world might be saved through technological transformations that have as their upshot not the salvation of humankind but its eradication, through its transformation or replacement, masquerading as the relief of the human condition.

Other people fancy that the world could be saved through political transformation, as if everybody could be made good if only we, who are not yet that good, could set the system straight first. Ambitions like these are always envisioned on a global scale nowadays; their advocates call themselves global citizens even though that's a contradiction in terms.

But I have learned a few things from superhero stories: First, if some scientist promises to bring all humankind peace and joy through the application of some technology, it means he's the bad guy; second, global governance is for supervillains; and third, reboots disappoint.

To conclude, I recommend Thor as a role model, but interpreted metaphorically to apply to us on a human scale, relevant to us living in a society of equals, enjoying freedoms in private and responsibilities in public. It would be too much to end by offering as encouragement that Valhalla awaits, but too grim to point out that Hel awaits us otherwise. The helmet, hammer, and bulging muscles are optional.

The cape, however, is recommended. If you can pull it off.